A Star
SHATTERED

THE RISE & FALL & RISE OF WRESTLING DIVA

TAMMY "Sunny" SYTCH

For more information contact:
Riverdale Avenue Books
5676 Riverdale Avenue
Riverdale, NY 10471.

www.riverdaleavebooks.com

Design by www.formatting4U.com
Cover by Scott Carpenter

Digital ISBN 978-1-62601-256-1
Print ISBN 978-1-62601-257-8
First Edition February 2016

This Book Is Dedicated to:

Chris, my one true love and soulmate;
My father, who made me the woman I am today
Stacey, my niece and soul sister, my fallen angel.

TABLE OF CONTENTS

PROLOGUE

Bruised. Battered. Broken ribs. Busted Lip.
Broken.

These are the physical feelings I have right now as I sit here, in an 8 x 8' cinderblock cell in the Mental Health Unit of the York Correctional Institution in Niantic, CT.

All that surrounds me are four walls of concrete, painted a not-so-lovely shade of lavender, a sink, a toilet, a shower with no privacy, and a "Bunkie" who has enough of her own emotional instabilities to not be bothered with my shit. At the rate her brain is functioning, she probably couldn't understand my shit anyway.

I'm lying under my hospital green sheet and blanket, excited that I received this writing tablet from the commissary today. Yes, that is a highlight of your week when you're an inmate at a women's state prison.

Inmate # 393257, to be exact.

You're probably wondering why I'm here, right? Well, to put it plainly, the man I loved most in the world, and whom I thought loved me, put me here. Yep, my fiancé... Damien.

The man I was going to marry.

Just 29 short days ago, he put a ring on my finger and asked me to be his wife. I said yes.

1

Why the hell did I say yes? Was it because I truly did love him? Was it because it was the first time I've ever been officially proposed to? Was it just that the sex was so good that I didn't want to let it go?

Maybe it was a combination of the three, because he really didn't have much else going for him.

He was one of the sexiest men I've ever been with. The way his curly long hair would blow in the breeze; the way his smooth, caramel skin felt against mine. The way he would saunter up to me sensually when he wanted to make love, his big green eyes sparkling when he looked at me. It was enough to make me melt.

On the other hand, he lived in a pigsty of a dumpy apartment, held a job (barely) at a home restoration company making $10.50 per hour, and his one, and only, credit card was still being managed by his Mommy. He was always behind on rent, and each time I moved back in, I had to clear up his bills.

So, who was this man I loved so much? He is the man that has broken me down emotionally so much that I feel physically numb. I feel nothing whatsoever. I'm sitting here in a tiny jail cell, and I'm not even that distraught.

I have my moments where I'll break down and lose it a little, especially when most meals consist of cream of wheat and white bread, or "slop" as they call it.

I'm numb. But, deep down, there are still feelings swimming beneath the surface.

Heartbroken. Cheated. Lied to. Betrayed. Used. Abused. Degraded. Demeaned. Brutalized. Hurt. Ashamed. Embarrassed.

In a word, shattered.

CHAPTER 1
THE BABY STEPS

"Behold I send you out as sheep amidst the wolves; so be shrewd as serpents and innocent as doves"
Matthew 10:16

This scripture from the New Testament is easily my favorite because it applies to every aspect of my life, especially now.

I've never felt more like a sheep amidst wolves as I do now. I'm in prison. My life has fallen apart. My freedom is gone. Everything I own is in the possession of the man who put me here.

A man. A man I had planned to marry.

I never thought a man whom I've known for less than a year could have such control over my life. It's pathetic and I'm ashamed of myself, and this coming from a woman who has been headstrong, confident, and assertive all her life. I allowed this man to do this to me, to put me in this miserable place, to take my life from me.

Things used to be different.

I was born Tamara Lynn Sytch, 7 lbs., 6 oz., on December 7th, 1972, to Raymond and Noreen, a steelworker and a homemaker, respectively. My father owned a steel fabrication and construction company, while my Mom was perfectly content staying at home raising my two sisters, my brother, and me.

We lived in a doublewide mobile home in a mid-sized town in New Jersey called Old Bridge. Yep, a trailer park. To this day, I still don't understand why we lived in a trailer, since Dad owned his own company. We always had everything we needed or wanted especially me because I was the baby so I can only chalk up our living arrangements to laziness.

Dad always walked around with about $500 cash rolled up in the pocket of his navy blue work pants, and quite often I was sent to the store to buy a gallon of milk with a $50 bill and was told to keep the change. Needless to say, I was Daddy's little girl. Actually, I was from the very moment I was born.

My father was retired Navy, so I was born in an Army hospital because of his benefits. I was to be named Jennifer Lynn, but that changed while my mother was in labor.

See, my father was a bit of a drinker in his younger years. The fact that his wife, at 38 years old, was in labor for 36 hours with their fourth child on the way 16 years since their third child was born put him over the edge a little. He was drinking and driving all over the Army base, and I mean all over all over the curbs, the grass, bushes, everywhere. The military police finally caught up with this mad man to arrest him, but when he explained the circumstances, they rushed him into the delivery room, out of pity, I suppose.

As my father rushed into delivery, drunk as a skunk, I was just coming out of the womb, and he proclaimed, "She's not Jennifer! She's Tamara!" as he waved the bottle of vodka he was drinking in the air with pride. Well, the vodka was aptly named "Tamara."

There I was, daddy's little girl from the first second of my life.

I was truly spoiled rotten, given anything and everything. I went fishing, crabbing, and hunting with Daddy. I went to amusement parks every weekend with my sisters and shopping daily with my Mom. There was nothing I ever needed because I had it all.

I was around 7 or 8 years old when my neighbor Joseph came over on a Saturday morning and wanted to watch TV because he said his parents wouldn't let him watch at home. Joseph was just a year older than me, but we were play buddies since we were born. He turned on local channel 11 (no one had cable TV back then) and guess what came on the screen?

WWF WRESTLING!

Now, I had never watched it before, nor did I know who any of the wrestlers were, but within a few short weeks I knew every wrestler, every weight, every town they hailed from, the good guys, the bad guys, the announcers, the referees everything! It was like crack for a 7-year-old kid. I couldn't get enough. It didn't take long until my Mom and my sister began taking me to live shows at the Meadowlands in North Jersey, each and every month. I was hooked!

I had every monthly wrestling magazine that was on the market; there must have been about 25 at the time, when you counted all of *Pro Wrestling Illustrated* titles, *WWF Magazine*, *Wrestling Eye*, *Wrestling Fury*, and so many more. I had every LJN rubber action figure as well, from Hulk Hogan to S.D.

"Special Delivery" Jones. But the highlight of my month was seeing the WWF live, seeing all my favorites: Ricky "the Dragon" Steamboat, Ivan Putski, Barry Windham, "Mr. Wonderful" Paul Orndorff, and most of all, the Hulkster!

Before a show one night, we hit the Howard Johnson's by Newark Airport for a pre-show dinner, and OH MY GOD! We got a lot more than dinner! A *whole* lot more! It turned out that the HoJo's at the airport was the hotel where all the boys stayed. I couldn't believe my eyes when I saw each and every one of the WWF crew walk through the lobby, sit and eat dinner in the same restaurant that we were OH MY FREAKIN GOD! I was in sheer heaven.

Luckily, my sister carried her camera everywhere, so I was getting photos and autographs galore. I was never turned down by anyone, probably because I was raised to be a sweet and polite kid. Month after month we hit the HoJo's for a good three or four autographs. I racked up a photo album and autograph collection that would have been the envy of the biggest superfan in the world!

At one show, the main event was Hulk Hogan vs. Sgt. Slaughter for the title Now, I was the biggest Hulkamaniac ever, so I made sure my Mom got our seats directly on the entranceway railing, which she usually always did anyway.

So it's time for the main event, and Hogan and Slaughter are battling like gladiators. Hulk got out of Sarge's finishing maneuver, the Cobra Clutch, a few times, but he got busted open in the course of the match. After Hulk got the win, as he was returning to the locker room, I patted him on the shoulder. When I looked at my hand, it was covered in his blood! Now, most 11-year-old girls would have screamed or cried, but I was so ecstatic that I made a hand print on the back of the program. That made my night. OMG! Hogan's blood! Yes! (OK, I was a demented child.). That same night, the WWF Women's Champion Wendi Richter (another fave) was defending her title against Leilani Kai, so I brought a bouquet of flowers for her that night. After her victory, and as the sound of Cyndi Lauper's "Girls Just Wanna Have Fun" hit the arena speakers, Wendi proceeded down the aisle and I reached over the railing with flowers in hand. Not only did she take them, but she gave me the biggest hug ever!

Needless to say, I was the envy of every single fan in my ringside vicinity. Blood from Hulk and a hug from Wendi. This was as good as things got for a superfan like me.

I have to credit Wendi Richter for inspiring me to get into the wrestling business at such a young age. Once I had a strong female role model to look up to, I started lifting weights, eating healthy, memorizing promos from TV, and practicing my "wrestling move repertoire." I had my Mom buy me elbow and knee pads, put on my old gymnastics leotard, tied neon-colored bandanas around my wrists and ankles, and even chose my entrance music: "Warrior" by Patti Smyth. My ring name was "The American Dream," Tammy Walker. OK, don't ask me how I came up with that one, I really had no clue.

So, I would cue my music, get all dressed and ready and make my entrance down the hallway to my parents' bedroom, or what I would call "My Arena."

Their bed was my ring, and the vast array of maneuvers and moves I would lay upon my invisible opponent was quite impressive. Dropkicks, elbow drops, camel clutches, figure four leg locks, you name it, at 11 years old, I knew my shit.

I started to phase out of my wrestling obsession around age 13, and my last live show was actually an AWA show in Asbury Park, NJ. On this night I completely fell in love for the first time with a 21-year-old beautiful man with dirty blonde hair and a killer smile, the one and only Shawn Michaels. After that night, I started to watch a little more of the AWA on TV; those were the "Wrestle Rock Rumble" days. I followed him in magazines because the AWA didn't run shows very often in New Jersey, so it was love from afar. Of course, I figured I would probably never, ever meet him or see him again... or so I thought!

CHAPTER 2
MY FIRST LOVE

"Silhouette, of a perfect frame, shadows of your smile will always remain" Avant

So now it's the late 1980's and I'm in my glorious high school years. Puberty hit and I wasn't really interested in wrestling anymore. I was more interested in my school activities and boys. My high school resume was quite impressive: captain of the cheerleading team, student council, National Honor Society, student of the month, ski club, peer leader, special-ed swim instructor, yearbook editor, Future Business Leaders of America, homecoming and prom queen nominee... the list goes on. I was also a straight-A student and ranked 19th out of 354 students academically in my class. Yeah, I was one of those goody two shoes nerds. But I was the HOT goody two shoes nerd; blond hair, big time flirt, with the shortest cheerleading skirt on the entire team. Yeah, I made sure of that.

I got my fair share of attention from the boys, but didn't have many boyfriends because I intimidated just about all of them. I may have been the biggest flirt of the school, but I was also probably the only virgin left in the place. That was by choice though, not lack of offers.

It was June of my senior year June 2, 1990 to be exact less than a month away from graduation. I was babysitting for my cousin Cara's newborn that night, when I got a phone call from my sister, Denise. She told me there was a small wrestling show in the high school gym, and a man she knew from back in our wrestling fan days, Professor Elliott Maron, was going to be there as the timekeeper. It sounded like fun, so I told her to go to the show, and when Cara came home, I'd head back down and see if I could join her there.

By the time I got there, the show was almost over, but I sat down and looked up at the ring. Almost instantly, I fell in love. There was a muscled-up, bleached blonde wearing white trunks with a standout tan. Wow. This guy was my exact type! I was 17 at the time, and I knew he must have been much older, but I kept joking with my Mom and sister, saying, "See that guy in the white? I'm gonna take him home tonight." They laughed it off, but I wasn't kidding.

I was thinking of some way to at least meet him, and since I've always been a creative girl, I had something in mind. I told my Mom and sis to go ahead home, since I had my own car there, and I was going to wait around a bit after the show.

So I waited. And waited. And as the locker room emptied and he came walking by, I very smoothly asked, "Can I have your autograph?"

Slick, huh?

He writes on the little piece of paper I handed him, and he handed it back. It read:

"Chris Candido"

And his phone number SCORE! I knew I was irresistible that night in my sexy white outfit and flowing blonde hair.

So he walked on and went out to the parking lot. I followed a few seconds later and got into my car. I noticed him sitting on the curb with his bag beside him. So, thinking quickly, I lowered the top of my 1989 Chevy Cavalier Z-24 white convertible, drove up to him in a slow and deliberate way, peered out over the door and in my sexiest 17 year old sex-kitten voice asked, "Do you need a ride?"

Man, I had all the lines that night.

He said his car was around the back of the gym, but he was waiting on his friends who must have left already. I told him to get in and that I would drive him around back to his car, which was a 1980 Monte Carlo, primer grey and, as Jim Ross would say, bowling shoe ugly. Not exactly the type of car my usual boys of choice would drive. See, in my school, the parking lot was full of sports cars, convertibles, BMWs, and Corvettes. Not broken down old Chevys.

So we pulled up next to his car, I parked, and we start to talk. I tell him I'm 17, about to graduate high school, and I'm going to the University of Miami on an academic scholarship to be a doctor.

He responds that he's 23, didn't get passed the 10th grade, and is an alcoholic, regularly going to AA meetings, and that he just got out of jail.

WHOA! OK!! The thought now going through my mind just changed from "Wow, is he cute," to "Oh my God, how do I get this alcoholic criminal psycho out of my car before he steals it, rapes me, or worse?"

He must have been able to tell by the look on my

face that I was scared half to death, so he broke down, started laughing, and said, to my relief, "I'm 18 and about to graduate from Red Bank Catholic High School. I'm not an alcoholic and I've never been to jail."

I had to have sighed out loud because at that moment, he grabbed the back of my head, pulled me in, and kissed me. He kissed me hard. It was easily the greatest kiss I had ever been given up to that point. When it ended, he apologized and said, "I'm sorry, I just had to."

"Don't be sorry," I replied. "Just do it again."

So he did. And he did. Again and again. Probably for about 30 minutes or so.

Those 30 minutes felt like the world had stopped, time stood still, and we were the only people left on the earth. It was absolutely magical.

Once again in my sex-kitten voice, I asked if he'd like to come over for a while. Of course, he said yes.

Chris followed me home, which was only about two miles away, and he followed me up the walkway, up the front steps, and through the door of my parents' house. My father was already asleep, so I rounded the corner to the kitchen where I heard my Mom and sister's voices. "I'm home," I announced. "And I brought someone with me." The look on their faces was priceless! They could not believe that I did what I said I'd do, and brought home the wrestler I said I would. I introduced them to him, and then Chris and I went to my bedroom to hang out.

Now, it's 1990, I'm 17 ½ years old, and I'm still a virgin. Yeah, I had my fair share of boyfriends, but I never gave it up. It was never right. So Chris and I talked for a while, watched TV, and made out

12

excessively. Ok, yeah, I blew him. But no sex. What kind of a girl do you think I am? OK, don't answer that question.

We stayed up until about 4:00 a.m. and I led him back to the Garden State Parkway so he could make his way home. I was head over heels in love, L-O-V-E, love! This was the first time I ever felt that way in my life. Christopher was my first love, even though I only knew him for a few hours.

The next day, we spoke on the phone all day long, and I invited him over again that night. When he got there, it was like we had been dating for a year already; everything was so perfect and right.

That night, June 3, 1990, was a monumental night for me well, for both of us. We made love. OK, we had beautiful sex, for the very first time, for the both of us. Turns out we were both virgins at 17 and 18 years old. I was, because of choice; he was because he was incredibly shy around girls, and girlfriends were always the last thing on his mind. Wrestling was first and foremost, followed by weightlifting. Those were his passions, his two true loves. And now I was his third true love.

For two people who really had no idea what they were doing in the sex department, it was really good. Our bodies moved together at the right pace with the right rhythm. It was only the missionary position, but it was perfect. It lasted about five minutes and it was the very first time I had an orgasm because of someone else. I had been masturbating for about six years, so I had them on my own, but none of my boyfriends ever got me to the point of no return. Granted, there was plenty of finger action and oral

13

play, but let's face it: teenage boys are pretty clueless as to what it takes to get a girl to that point.

But Chris and I were just physically made for each other. There was never a time when I didn't have an orgasm from having sex with him. He was also the best kisser I had ever had—and I had kissed quite a few frogs looking for my prince.

So that was it. June 2 became our anniversary, and June 3 became our "fucking anniversary," pun intended.

The next day in school, I walked around like a proud peacock, bragging to all my girls that I wasn't the "last American virgin" anymore. They laughed at it, because most of them lost their virginity by the 10th grade. So maybe I was a prude in a way, but I could give a blowjob that could win awards! So there!

That was the beginning a relationship that lasted almost 16 years. Everything moved so fast. Within two months, on August 10, I was supposed to leave for school in Miami. I had my U-Haul rented and a hitch put on my Z-24. I knew my roommate and we discussed who was bringing what to the dorm. Everything was in place and college was waiting … until …

August 5, 1990. I broke down. I knelt in front of my dad on the living room floor as he sat in his recliner and I cried.

"What's wrong, Squirt?" he asked. Squirt was my dad's nickname for me since I was a baby.

"I can't go to Miami, Daddy," sobbed. "I love Chris and I want to stay here with him."

My dad looked at me sternly and said, in his strong voice, "Then don't go. You're giving up a scholarship, but if you don't want to go, don't."

There was a sense of disappointment in the tone

of his voice, but I could see that gleam in his eyes, the gleam that gave him away. He was happy I wasn't going. He was as happy as a pig in shit that his baby girl wasn't driving 1,200 miles away and spending four years away from him.

I was Daddy's little girl. All he wanted was for me to be happy. He gave me anything I wanted and did anything for me. It would have broken his heart for the little girl who made his lunch for work every day and played the piano for him to fall asleep to leave home for that long, that far away.

I called Chris and told him I was staying home. I think he was crying on the other end of the phone!

We spent the rest of the summer lounging on the beach, soaking up the sun and soaking in each other's company. In September I enrolled in Brookdale Community College, since I had turned down Rutgers University, the only local university I had applied. For the rest of the year, we carried on like two giddy lovebirds, hopelessly in love. I was going to college and he was wrestling his indie shows, and I was there for every single one of them.

Within a few weeks of dating, he was a permanent fixture at my house four or five nights a week, staying over all of those nights, although Daddy had no idea. If Daddy had known we were sharing a bed five nights a week, his big, booming Russian voice would have cowered me into a corner, and his big, strong Russian palm would have slapped Chris so hard he would have flown across the room with one swat.

He never knew.

Until one night.

At around 3:00 a.m., Chris got hungry so he

wrapped himself in a towel and tiptoed into the kitchen. We had a huge pantry, and a light came on when the pantry doors were opened. Chris cracked open the pantry doors and scanned over the food and junk food packed inside, everything from potato chips to cookies to Entenmann's cakes. The plan was to grab something fast and retreat back to my bedroom.

"Hungry?"

My father's big, gravelly voice boomed out, nearly scaring Chris out of his towel. He was caught! In the kitchen at 3:00 a.m. Wearing nothing but a towel! The shit was about to hit the fan.

Chris gaped at my father, a deer caught in the headlights.

"Go start up the grill," my father commanded.

Chris did as he was told and went outside, in a towel and bare feet, in 45 degree weather, at 3:00 in the morning, and lit the grill.

My father pulled out a dozen filet mignons from the freezer, handed them to Chris, and told him to put them on the grill and don't come back in until they were fully cooked. So Chris goes outside and practically freezes his balls off for 20-30 minutes cooking up 12 2-inch thick steaks.

When everything was cooked, he came back inside with the steaks, and my dad has a smorgasbord of food lined up on the kitchen table, enough to feed an army. Potato salad, macaroni salad, cole slaw, the works.

He made Chris sit down. Dad took four steaks for himself and gave the other eight to Chris.

"You said you were hungry, now eat," my father said, as he spooned heaps of salads onto Chris' plate, alongside about 40 ounces of juicy filet mignon.

By this point, Chris was relieved he hadn't been shot, but he was still white as a ghost in fear. My dad could be a scary man. He stood 6'3", weighed 360 pounds, and had hands the size of bear claws. I once saw him make a grown man break down and cry.

There was nothing else Chris could do except pick up his fork and knife and eat. He ate, and ate, and ate, for about an hour straight, until all the steaks were gone, and all the salads were gone, too.

The entire time, while doing his best to not vomit, he tried to keep up conversation and give respectful answers to all of my Dad's small talk questions. "Yes, sir." "No, sir." "Yes, sir."

I had been hiding in my room the whole time, terrified to even peek my head out of the door to see what's going on, so was clueless about Dad and Chris' late-night buffet. About two hours after he had snuck out of my room to grab a snack, he returned, just as the morning sun was coming up.

"Oh my God! What happened?" I asked. "Is he pissed?"

Chris looked at me, with a thoroughly confused expression on his face.

"He fed me," he said. "A lot."

I squealed with joy. "That means he LIKES you," I said. "Ohmigod, I am so happy he likes you!" And I hugged him like I hadn't seen him in years.

See, this was my Dad's test. He was testing Chris' will and respect. And Chris passed, with flying colors. After that, we didn't have to hide his car around the corner anymore and sneak him in the back door. He was now part of the family.

Thank God.

CHAPTER 3
A LONG, HOT SUMMER

So Christopher and I began our journey into our relationship throughout the remainder of 1990 and into the spring of 1991. These months were dotted with many independent bookings for him up and down the eastern seaboard. Of course, his devoted girlfriend went with him everywhere.

Already an avid photographer, I began shooting his matches while my video camera was set up somewhere filming. One way or another, my photographs landed in the hands of the very well-known magazine editor Bill Apter and he asked me to do some freelance work for him.

Awesome! This was going to be easy money. I just had to shoot the matches I was at with Chris, then get paid for it!

Not exactly.

I did shoot the matches. Then I had to get the prints developed, and then send them to Bill. Then he picked which pictures he wanted to use in the dozen or so magazines he edited. Then he sent me a check for $10 for each photo used.

By the time I spent money on buying film and

getting six rolls or so developed, I usually broke even, and sometimes I lost money on the deal.

But I did get photo credit and one of my shots did make it to a color centerfold! (That pic was of a tarred and feathered Ricky Morton. I can still see that picture in my head! It was a great shot!)

That was my first paying job in the wrestling business. I thought it would be my only one, since I was elbow deep in biology books by then, but that wasn't to be.

Chris got booked on a show run by Joel Goodhart in the Tri-State Wrestling Alliance. Chris wanted me to escort him to the ring as his valet, but Joel said there was no way he was paying someone who wasn't in the business to valet on his show.

So I wasn't going to get paid. No big deal, this was for Chris anyway.

I was 17 and all excited that I was actually going to "work" on my first pro wrestling show. Whoooo Hooooo!!

I went to the mall and bought this fancy dress, white lace, off the shoulder, with ostrich feathers on the shoulders and shoes and jewelry to match. I must have spent $200 to work a show I was making nothing on, but I was so excited, I didn't care.

We had one of Chris' friends do an impromptu photo shoot before the show so there would be actual photographic proof that it actually happened.

Off to the Philadelphia Civic Center we go. On the card were Abdullah the Butcher, Woman, Kevin Sullivan, Baby Doll (who took a bump while six months pregnant), Magnum TA, and a host of Pennsylvania and New Jersey independent guys who no one had ever heard of, including the Sandman and the Rockin' Rebel.

Chris was scheduled to be in a match with all the indie guys, a reverse steel cage battle royal. What is that, you ask? Well, all the guys start on the floor on the outside of the cage, and the winner is the first to climb and get into the cage.

Stupid. Yes, I know.

But I was all excited while I was getting ready. Nancy Sullivan, better known as Woman, started making small talk with me. "So, are you a heel or face?" she asked. I froze. I had no friggin' clue what she meant.

By this time, I was smartened up to the business somewhat, but right then I realized I had a lot more to learn.

Since I looked confused, she clarified.

"Babyface or heel?"

I finally caught on and nervously replied, "Oh, babyface. I'm sorry."

I had just made a complete ass of myself with the very first real "name" I'd met in the business, and I found the first opportunity I could to sneak out of the room in embarrassment.

Nancy was a very, very lovely woman, and I'm sure she didn't think any less of me for being so green. She probably likened it to her early days as the Fallen Angel, valet to the maniacal Kevin Sullivan in the early 1980's.

We ran into each other on a few indies after that and always maintained a nice rapport. Unfortunately, the world lost beautiful Nancy just a few years ago at the hands of her husband, Chris Benoit. That tragedy will never be forgotten.

Neither will Nancy. RIP.

The next big show on Chris' agenda was an indie card for Dennis Corraluzzo's NWA in South Jersey. Headlining the card would be "Hot Stuff" Eddie Gilbert and God-knows who else, it was so long ago. Eddie took an instant liking to Chris, but it was obvious he took a liking to me as well. He was very nice, posed for a few pics for me, and we made some small talk.

The next thing we know, Chris started getting phone calls from Dennis saying that Jerry "The King" Lawler wanted him down in Memphis in the USWA, on Eddie Gilbert's recommendation.

OH MY GOD! This would be his first full-time wrestling job in an actual territory with television exposure!

It was a dream come true for Chris. He was more excited than a kid in a candy store.

Of course, being the ever-supportive girlfriend, I agreed to come along. Since it was over the summer, months before my first year in college, I wouldn't be missing any school, so I got my parents' blessing. We packed up his 1980 Chevy Monte Carlo with some clothes and a cooler of food, and hit the road for our 19-hour journey to good ol' Memphis, Tennessee!

About 17 hours in, and only 130 miles or so from Graceland, his car died. It just died. It was 98 degrees of sweltering heat somewhere in Tennessee and we were stuck on the side of the road. Keep in mind it was a Friday night and Chris was supposed to start that very next day in the Memphis Coliseum.

Shit! What the hell do we do? Luckily, we found a gas station close by, and they agreed to fix Chris' car at 6:00 a.m. the following morning. It turned out the water pump went kaput. They replaced it in a few hours, and we were back on the road.

As we pulled up to the Coliseum that hot and sticky Saturday afternoon, we were greeted in the parking lot by a scrawny, dirty looking man who looked like he'd slept in a gutter the night before. It was Downtown Bruno, a Memphis heel manager who would later gain fame as Harvey Wippleman in the WWF.

Bruno told us that the ring wasn't up yet, and that there was no air conditioning in the building, so he directed us to go to the resident Memphis motel and get our room. As we pulled up to the Admiral Benbow Inn, we noticed the vacancy sign read "$19/night." Holy cow! Memphis is cheap!

As we entered the room, we immediately realized why it was so cheap. The bed was completely sunken in the middle; it was like the springs had been removed. The blue carpets were so stained they were more of a very dark gray.

Since we were so sweaty from the breakdown and the 19-hour drive, I decided to take a shower. When I came out and began to dress, I realized that the filth from the carpet had made my feet even dirtier than they were before I went into the shower! Ewww!

Being the spoiled, bratty 17-year-old that I was, I insisted we leave. We found the Howard Johnson's down the road for $40 bucks.

By now, it was time to head to the show. As we pulled up to the arena, another car pulled up alongside us, a huge brown Cadillac packed with a very interesting cast of characters. At the wheel was a terribly ugly, scarred-up guy with long black hair, messed up teeth, and wearing a turban. In the passenger seat was an athletically built guy with a dark blonde ponytail who happened to resemble a certain action movie hero. And taking up most of the back seat was a guy with long curly brown hair, a pot belly, and a dimply smile that only a mother could love, wearing jean overalls.

These three men turned out to be Sabu, Rob Van Dam, and Tex Salinger (who was later known as Phineas Godwin and Mideon in the WWF.) It was their first crack at the "big-time" too, and we all instantly became friends.

Especially Sabu. He and Chris really hit it off, and since he is highly respectful towards women, so did we.

This was the start of Chris' run with the USWA. When your boys on the indie scene talk about "paying their dues," most of them honestly don't know what that expression really means. Working the USWA was paying your dues. You got paid anywhere from $15 to $40 per night, six nights a week, and the $40 only happened once a week, on Monday nights in Memphis, the BIG show. Even in 1990, that pay was only enough to pay for gas to get you to the next town, which was between three and six hours away. How were you to pay for a hotel and food?

I don't know how some other guys did it, but luckily for us, I had a very generous father who didn't want his little girl sleeping in a car and starving to death. I bought an electric burner and a pot and cooked some meals in our hotel room at times.

Times were definitely tough, and I was not used to living this way, but it gave Chris the priceless experience of working with guys the likes of Eddie Gilbert, Jerry Lawler, Bill Dundee, Tony Anthony, Tracy Smothers, and Eric Embry. I also became friends with Stacy Carter, who soon after became Jerry Lawler's wife and found fame of her own in the WWF as The Kat.

Once a week, the boys took a nine-hour bus ride to Dallas, Texas, for a TV taping. Girlfriends weren't allowed to go on the bus, so I stayed back in Memphis alone. Eddie Gilbert had heard that I was staying behind, as he always did, because he despised taking the bus ride, so he asked me to hang out with him, his brother Doug, Tony Anthony, and Eddie's childhood friend John Guillem (who was somewhat "off" if you know what I mean).

I joined them for Chinese food, followed by Putt Putt Golf, and headed to my motel to check in. When I got there, they refused to rent me a room, even though I had stayed there many times before.

Unbeknownst to me, Memphis had a law that stated that you had to be 18 to rent a hotel room.

Shit!

Chris was 18 and had always rented the room, but I was just 17. What the hell was I supposed to do? I drove back to Eddie's apartment and begged for help. We went back to the hotel and he asked for a room. The older woman working the desk must have thought I was a hooker or that Eddie was a pedophile, because she already knew I was 17 and Eddie's ID showed he was 31. The look on her face was worth a thousand words! Ha!

But at least I had a safe, warm place to sleep that night.

This became the weekly routine for our little Memphis crew—Chinese food, golf, Nintendo, and Eddie renting my room.

Thank God for Eddie and his friendship, or else I never would have survived.

In later years, when Jerry Lawler published his memoirs, I found out the REAL reason why Chris got the job in Memphis. Eddie had told Jerry of a sweet young blonde dating a kid with some decent in-ring talent. He didn't know exactly where this kid would fit in in Memphis, but he was damned sure he'd bring his blonde girlfriend with him.

Eddie and Jerry agreed that they could each work on getting the girl in bed—or maybe even the both of them. That sweet, young blonde was me.

And no, it didn't happen.

If you don't believe me, buy Jerry's book and read for yourself (You're welcome, King!)

Eddie and I remained great friends after our departure from Memphis, and Chris built a lifelong brotherhood with Sabu.

It was now back to college for me, and off to the indies for Chris.

CHAPTER 4
FORCES OF NATURE

There are some things in life we just can't control.

Like the weather, or our own destinies.

My destiny was all about to change without even giving me a hint to warning.

I was just about finished with my second year of college at Monmouth University—pre-med, majoring in biology. Chris was set to work another show for Dennis, but this time the one and only Jim Cornette was on the show.

Jim had a reputation for having an extremely hot temper and diarrhea of the mouth, but was also known for having one of the best minds in the business. He was a manager extraordinaire and worked with some of the best wrestlers ever to set foot in a ring.

Dennis told Jim to take a look at a young kid he had on the show—Chris. Jim, always on the lookout for new young talent for his company, Smoky Mountain Wrestling, happily obliged.

He liked what he saw. A lot. After the show, we all went out to a little rib place near the venue. Chris wasn't much of a conversationalist back then; he was usually too shy, especially when he was around other people in the business that he admired. But me, I was as perky and charming as ever.

Within a couple of weeks after that meeting, Chris was invited down to begin working for JC and SMW. Based out of Knoxville, Tennessee, this would mean another road trip for us. Since this promised to be more of a long-term spot, I had to figure out what to do about school. I applied as a transfer student to the University of Tennessee in Knoxville, home of the Volunteers. I had no doubt that I would be accepted; after all, I had a 4.0 GPA at Monmouth and UT wasn't that tough of a school to get into.

So once again, we packed up—both of our cars this time—and headed down to Knoxville.

We found an apartment fairly quickly, a beautiful modern complex called Concept 21 for a whopping $395 per month. In New Jersey, that apartment would have easily been $800 or more. Living expenses were very low in Tennessee. We settled in; I went to UT to register for classes, and we hit the road for Chris' first SMW tour.

In the USWA, we thought we had some long drives, driving for three hours each day. We weren't prepared for the Smoky Mountain hikes, which were regularly four to six hours per day, and usually those drives were into the winding roads of the Kentucky mountains.

For the first month, every time Chris stepped into the ring, the fans looked baffled. He was in there doing all his fast-moving, rope-running spots and occasional high-flying maneuvers. The SMW fans looked like they'd seen an alien. They were so used to the "old school" style of the likes of Ricky Morton and Tracy

Smothers, where a punch and a kick meant more than a moonsault. They didn't know how to respond to someone like Chris.

Ricky and Tracy eventually pulled him aside and "showed him the ropes" of how to work a match in the South for those fans. Once he slowed down and adjusted his style, and perfected his whiny, crybaby heel promos, he fit in nicely.

After that first month, we were invited to dinner by Jim Cornette and his wife at the time, Kelly. We were set to meet them at Calhoun's on the River, the best BBQ spot in Knoxville. We couldn't relax that whole day. If Jim was taking us out to dinner, he must have had something great to tell Chris about his career and his future in SMW.

So we sat down to dinner, order our meals, and Jim looked at me.

"I need a girl."

"Hmmm?" I responded with a mouth full of BBQ sauce.

"Just hear me out," Jim said. "I need a girl, a fresh face to be this Northern, bitchy college student. Someone nobody has ever seen before to be a heel manager. Someone to work ringside, cut promos. It'll only be for six months. You can go back to school after that."

WHOA Nelly! Slow down just a minute. As I began to process it all, I thought this guy must REALLY be nuts! I was a pre-med student, I was going to be a plastic surgeon. Wrestling was Chris' dream, not mine. I had never been on camera before. I wouldn't have the faintest idea what I was doing. I had been a cheerleader, so I was used to being in front of crowds, but being on camera? No, not me, thanks. Besides, there was no way in hell I was taking off six months from school for any reason.

Nevertheless, I agreed to give it a shot. I figured I could make a few bucks on the weekends and attempt to support myself, since I had been relying on money from my father up until then.

So the day came when I needed to film a couple of promos for a months' worth of TV, introducing myself and eventually my first protégé, "Prime Time" Brian Lee.

Brian was a huge guy, 6'6 and about 280 pounds, with long blond hair. Real nice guy, but dumb as a box of rocks and couldn't cut a promo if his life depended on it.

Enter: Moi.

Now I had never put a promo together before either, but I was gonna give it a whirl. Jim gave me four sheets of scripts, told me to be exact, take my time, do my best, and put everything into my own words. What Jim didn't realize was that part of the reason I was such a good student was because I had a photographic memory. I could read something once and give it right back to you, word for word.

So after about three minutes of looking over the sheet, I said I was ready to go. He gave me a look of disbelief, but he told the cameras to roll.

3, 2, 1…Action!

I gave him his promo word for word, with proper inflection and delivery, with good facials, without a hitch. That expression of disbelief slowly transformed into a look of excitement. Had he just stumbled across a diamond in the rough? His next big star?

He had. But I wasn't just his next big star. I was about to become the biggest heel in the company. Tammy Fytch, student from Wellesley College, a prissy private women's college in Massachusetts. Her idol? Hillary Clinton. Her objective? To rule over SMW with her prima donna feminist act, and to dominate every man in the territory.

It was perfect, a match made in heaven. Jim Cornette, Smoky Mountain Wrestling, and Tammy Fytch.

Boy, was I hated! You see, down in the Tennessee/ Kentucky area, the fans still believed in everything. There were no "smart marks." Kayfabe was alive and well. The more I opened my mouth each and every week, the more they hated me.

During a match between Chris and Brian and the Rock and Roll Express, I had to slap Ricky Morton. OH MY GOD! You would have thought I slapped the Pope by the fans' reaction! Every female, and most men, in that building wanted to rip my throat out and tear me from limb to limb. They would reach over the guardrail, which was just rope connected between two posts, and try their damnedest to grab a hold of me.

One night, one of them succeeded. As my "heat" was building even more and surpassing even Jim Cornette status, I was attacked by a rather burly woman—ok, she was a 400-pound beast with three teeth and spit flying out of her mouth with every nasty word she screamed in my direction.

We were in Barbourville, Kentucky, a rather "hick-filled" town, when Brian and I were leaving the ringside area. As we were halfway down the aisle to the locker room, out of the corner of my eye I saw a set of hands (ok, more like bear claws) reaching for my head. The next thing I knew, I was on the floor with this wildebeest next to me, her hands full of my hair. In a split second, I was being dragged across the floor by my hair. Brian had grabbed two fists full of her hair, while she still had my hair, and he was dragging both of us across the high school gym floor.

He finally got her to loosen her grip and I wriggled out of her grasp. Now, having the little temper that I do, I wasn't going away with my tail between my legs, so I got up, stormed into the locker room, grabbed the quite heavy championship belt, and bee-lined for her back in the gym. I was going to permanently imprint that belt across her face. Corny, rightly afraid that I was going to bash her face in with the belt, screamed to Brian.

"Dag gummit, Brian! Go get her before she kills someone!!"

Brian followed me out, and in one quick swoop, he picked me up under his arm so I was parallel with the floor, and he carried me off to the locker room.

I was furious!

And bright red!

And ready to kick some ass! Although I had never been in a fight in my entire life, I sure put on one hell of a believable act.

We hit some pretty interesting towns with some pretty interesting folks, to put it nicely.

Ok, who am I kidding? I'm not that nice and politically correct.

In the hills of Kentucky, you'd be lucky if the entire front row would make up one complete set of teeth. And it was blatantly obvious that there was quite a bit of "brotherly lovin'" going on up in those hills.

31

Incest was running rampant with the amount of deformities you'd see. One woman had no corneas or pupils in her eyes, her skin was purple, and she had three club-like stumps on each hand instead of five fingers. One man in Hazard, Kentucky, thought he was a dog and barked the entire night. There's some crazy shit you see up in those hills!

My first experience working with another girl was when they put Brian in a program with the "Dirty White Boy" Tony Anthony, and JC brought in his wife Kimberly to work with him.

Now, "Lil Kim," as Tony affectionately called her, hated me from Day One. She was so pissed that I was offered a job before she was, a spot she thought she was entitled to since she had been around the business longer than me.

What she was too stupid to understand that there was no way she could play my role, because she had been known in that area for a couple of years as Tony's regular valet in the USWA and the independents. And Tony was too thick in the skull to be able to explain that to her.

So we started our angle, and she took every opportunity she possibly could to get her hands on me and "stiff" me, one way or another. She'd pull my hair, scratch at my neck, kick my shins with her cowboy boots ... she was horrible.

I finally had to put my foot down and tell Cornette, "It's her or me. I've had enough. Either end this angle and get rid of her, or I quit"

He promised me that there were only two more weeks left in the program and that I wouldn't have to deal with her again after that. He promised she

32

wouldn't touch me again except for the match at the culmination of the angle, and even then it would be minimal. God knew he didn't want to lose his money maker, his number-one heel, Tammy Fytch.

The final match was booked as a mixed tag team match, and the losers were the team whose girl got stripped first. Just great… not only do I have to wrestle her, but she's going to be tearing my clothes off. Again, I protested to JC. Yes, I was quite the spoiled bitch back then.

He reassured me that there would be no wrestling and that I could get stripped any way I wanted.

Hmm…

Luckily for me, I have creativity coming out of every pore, so I cooked up a plan to get stripped "naked" in front of the fans without them seeing even one speck of skin.

The night arrived for the match and I was ready with layers and layers of clothing on. The bell rang, she stormed in and tore my sweatshirt off revealing a T-shirt that read, "I'm too smart to wear just that!" Next, she tore off that T-shirt, only to reveal another shirt which read, "Ha ha, I'm still dressed!" We rolled around a little as she pulled off my shorts, this time to reveal a pair of bike shorts. As she chased me around the ring, I scurried out of her reach and crawled under the ring, where she followed. I quickly removed my T-shirt, (I was wearing a sports bra) and bike shorts and gave them to her, as well as the bra I had taped to my stomach.

She then emerged from under the ring victorious, with my clothes and skivvies in hand—leaving me "butt naked" under the ring. Chris ran out to the ring with a huge quilt and threw it under the ring to me so I could cover up. I wrapped my "naked" self up in the quilt and Brian carried me over his shoulder, off into the sunset.

There. Done. Match won by the Dirty White Girl. Fans happy I got "stripped" naked. Even though they never saw a thing, they thought they did, and that's all that mattered.

Stupid hillbillies. They'd fall for anything.

I'm sure you figured out that Lil Kim and I never got along back then, but that was 1993. We were kids. Recently I found her on Facebook and we "buried the hatchet" after all these years.

Life is too short to have enemies.

Now keep in mind, JC promised me I would have a six-month run and be out of the business, but I was too natural on promos, too good at ringside, and gained tremendous heat too easily to be finished up so soon. We were now two-and-a-half years into my run and I was a senior at UT with just over one semester to graduate.

I was making $175 per weekend, and Chris was making $400, so together we were making a nice weekly salary, especially considering how affordable things were there. He and I managed to save up $12,000 in just over two years, which was quite good for a couple of 20 year-old kids.

I was doing well in school, mostly A's, and going to classes on Mondays, Tuesdays, and Wednesdays, and studying in the car and locker room Thursday through Sunday.

School was going great. And then, one evening, I got a phone call.

34

CHAPTER 5
DID I EVER TELL YOU YOU'RE MY HERO?

"Daddy died."

That's all I heard on the other end of the phone.

"Daddy's dead, Tam."

It was my brother, Raymond, with the most horrible two words a 20 year-old girl could ever hear.

Daddy's little girl.

I couldn't even respond. I just collapsed to the floor, sobbing. Sobbing became hysterics. Hysterics turned to shock.

My father, the man I spent my tomboy years with hunting, fishing, and crabbing, building tree houses with was gone.

The silent shock turned immediately to anger. Anger towards God.

"How could you do this?" I screamed out loud. "How could you take my Daddy from me? Fuck you, God! If there really was a God, you would have kept him here with me! FOR me!!"

Right then and there, I immediately lost all faith in God, Jesus, and religion as a whole.

When something that devastating happens so suddenly to someone as young as me, you need someone to blame. I blamed God.

Although God had nothing to do with it.

For a few years, my Dad was battling with congestive heart failure. That means fluid collects around your heart, puts a strain on it, and makes it difficult to breathe.

My Dad was 6'3", 360 pounds. His doctor told him to quit smoking, and he did, cold turkey. His doctor told him to lose weight. That was a bit more difficult.

You see, my dad's favorite thing in life was food, and eating food. Eating a lot of it. He didn't just eat for nutrition; he thoroughly enjoyed the act of eating. He would never sit and have one serving. He enjoyed his way through two or three servings at a time. He enjoyed spending money on lavish cuts of meat—hence the dozen filet mignons that were in the freezer the night Chris was caught in a towel at 3:00 a.m. Chris probably got off lucky; knowing my dad, there were probably three dozen filets in the freezer at a time.

And my Dad didn't care for "healthy" foods. Nevermind lean chicken and salads. He was Russian. He loved his beef, liver, gravies, sauces, potatoes, and especially butter and cheese! He used more butter than Paula Deen when he cooked! (This is most likely where I got my fixation with butter and cheese as well.)

I would make him healthy turkey sandwiches to take to work every day for lunch, trying to get him to lose some weight. I took care of my Daddy. He still went out to the grease truck for lunch at work every day anyway.

My Dad passed away of a massive heart attack at 6:00 p.m. on October 18, 1993. He had the heart attack during dinner. He was enjoying seafood takeout from his favorite fish place. He died while doing what he enjoyed the most.

I was crushed.

Devastated.

I could not believe this was happening. I was only 20 years old. I wasn't ready to lose my father. I was in Tennessee, 750 miles away from my Dad in New Jersey. I was so far away that there was nothing I could do; there was nothing I could do to help him.

I felt incredibly guilty. I still do. If only I could have been there. If only I wasn't doing this stupid wrestling thing in Tennessee... maybe I could have given him CPR and saved him. If only I was there.

The next morning, Chris and I flew home. My sister picked us up at the airport. I cried the whole flight home. When I got to the house, I went into a state of shock again. I was in total denial and disbelief. I ran through my parents' home, determined I was going to find my Daddy there, alive and well. I was calling out his name, anxiously hoping to hear him yell back, "Hey squirt, I'm in the basement."

He didn't yell back. He wasn't there.

I ran into his closet and grabbed some of his clothes, stole my mother's car keys, and took off for the hospital. I was SURE I could find him there.

I bolted into the ER, asking what room he was in. The nurse kept looking at the computer and looking up at me, not wanting to tell me what she had found. I told her that my brother told me he died the previous night. "I'm sorry, honey," she said. "He's probably in the morgue."

I knew the morgue must have been in the basement, so I found a service elevator to take me there. Tears were streaming down my face as my heart pounded with fear. I wasn't going to believe he was gone until I saw him for myself. I was crying, thinking it was all some horrible mistake. "He's OK, he has to be OK." The elevator doors opened to a cold, dark, gray hallway. At the end of the hall were two big white doors, and at the top of the doors hung a sign. MORGUE.

I found it. I found HIM! I had to break into the morgue, because for obvious reasons it isn't open to the public. But that wasn't stopping me.

I approached the lady at the desk and said, "Where's my father? I need to see my father! I need to bring him home.

She asked his name and I stuttered, "Raymond Sytch," choking on my tears.

"I'm sorry honey, you can't see him," she said. "They haven't cleaned him up yet. There's all tubes and…"

I broke down. Tubes? Tubes coming out of my father?

It must have been true.

My Daddy was gone.

My mom eventually found me and took me to my doctor, actually my pediatrician. He gave me a prescription for 20 Valium to help me get through the next couple of days. Each Valium hit me like a ton of bricks and I slept most of the time leading up to the funeral.

My Dad was one of a kind. A stubborn, strong-willed big bear of a Russian man. Navy retired. Blind in one eye from his service in the Navy.

My dad would never curse. He didn't have to. Just the tone of his voice was enough to make you behave. The worst curse word that ever came out of his mouth was "shit."

He was extremely generous and would do anything or give anything to his family or friends. There was never anything I wanted or needed since I got everything I asked for and more.

My Dad never sounded happy when I would talk about SMW shows. He always called it "that stupid wrestling stuff you are doing." He would dismiss it as some hobby that I couldn't possibly take seriously.

What I didn't know, and I found out after his death, is that he would go to the corner news stand by his business, sit on a milk crate, and flip page by page through the two dozen different wrestling magazines that they carried looking for my picture or even the slightest mention of my name.

He bought every issue.

He was proud of his little girl. He liked to brag to his employees and friends about me.

I never knew all this while he was alive. I never got to smile at him looking at me proudly and to say "thank you."

Unfortunately my Dad passed long before I could REALLY make him proud, long before I made my way to the WWF. He never got to see me perform on the big stage, on pay-per-views, in glossy color magazines instead of black and white.

I take that back. He saw. He has the best seat in the house. And he watches over me always. I know he does.

I love you Daddy.

I miss you.

CHAPTER 6
A TWIST OF FATE

Chris and I returned to Knoxville after the funeral and I tried to continue life as usual, but I couldn't. I was so grief-stricken and depressed that my grades started to fall in school. I was eventually failing organic chemistry, so I opted to drop the class and accept an incomplete instead of an "F."

I attended the subsequent semesters on a part-time basis. I was just so devastated by my father's death that I couldn't concentrate. I couldn't focus.

My work, however, was thriving. I continued to garner the most heat in the company and I was voted number-two in the Best Manager category in the *Wrestling Observer Newsletter* year-end awards in 1993 (right behind my mentor, Jim Cornette). JC even placed a photocopy of it in my paycheck envelope with a note reading, "If you continue to get more heat than me, you're fired."

He was joking, of course.

This was an obvious compliment of a job well done, but it still didn't earn me a raise, damn it!

1994 was off to a good start. I was working on dealing with the death of my father, school was fine, and work was brilliant. Chris and I had made

Knoxville our home and had no intentions of moving back to New Jersey in the foreseeable future.

On December 4, the phone rang in our apartment. I answered.

"Tammy? Hi, this is Bruce Prichard from the WWF calling. How are you today?"

"Fine, thanks," I answered. "Can you hold on a second?"

I covered the phone with my hand and yelled for Chris to come into the living room. "The WWF is calling for you," I whispered, pointing at the phone. Apparently I need to work on my whispering, because Bruce heard me on the other end of the line.

"No, actually, I'm calling for you," he said. "We'd like to know if you would like to come up to Stamford for an audition."

"An audition? Sure!"

He told me that someone from the travel department would be calling me and we ended the conversation.

An audition with the WWF, on Monday, December 7... my birthday! Could I have asked for a better birthday present?

But wait, an audition for what? Now I was stumped. Maybe I should have asked him that question when I had him on the phone.

Regardless, Chris and I started jumping for joy. I was headed to the WWF headquarters on my birthday for an audition. They must have seen a tape or two of my Smoky Mountain stuff and wanted to see me live.

So I packed an overnight bag and prepared for my trip. I couldn't sleep the entire weekend. I was so anxious I couldn't sit still.

41

Monday came. My 21st birthday. That wasn't important though, because as a young adult who was abstinent from alcohol, turning 21 was just another day. But I was on a 6:00 a.m. flight, headed to LaGuardia airport, where a big, black limo was sent to pick me up and take me to the Marriott in Stamford. This was my first real limo ride, with the exception of my junior and senior proms, which really don't count. I was overcome with excitement. How much better could this get?

I was taken to the Titan TV studios. As I walked in, I was greeted by a few of the staff and then ushered up to the make-up room. I met the most wonderful lady there. Flaming red hair, big blue eyes, and tons of freckles. She introduced herself as Jill Getlan, make-up artist.

Make-up artist extraordinaire would be more like it! In a mere 30 minutes, she turned this low maintenance college girl who never wore much make-up into a glamour-puss sex symbol, fit for any movie screen. Jill quickly became one of my best friends and confidants.

They then brought me down to the studio, an empty, cold, dark studio with one camera set up and a backdrop. What in the world was going on?

A producer came in and said, "Hi, nice to meet you. We're going to have you read from the teleprompter and we'll be all done."

What? Read from the tele...who? All done? Wait, what exactly is going on?

I excused myself and said, "I'm sorry, but I think there's been a mistake. I'm a heel manager. I work ringside. I don't even know what a teleprompter is."

"Don't worry, you'll be fine," he said. "Just read the words as they scroll down the monitor under the camera lens."

Ok, if you insist.

They counted me down and the words started to scroll. They all kind of blurred together. I'm not sure if that was because I was so nervous, or if they were moving too fast for me. My palms were sweaty, my heart was racing, and my temperature rose even though the studio was so cold. I must have been nervous.

But wait! I don't GET nervous! I never had, about anything. What the hell was happening to me now? I didn't even get nervous for my first SMW promo! WTF?

I started to read. And stumbled. And stuttered. And mispronounced words. And stumbled some more. At one point I just stopped entirely.

It had to be the single most embarrassing, terrible, horrific audition any that studio crew had ever seen.

When I was done, just ten short minutes later, I was whisked away to my awaiting limo and taken back to the Marriott, where I would spend the night and fly home the next morning.

I got to my room, dropped my bag, and shut the door. I walked straight over to the phone, stone-faced, picked it up, and dialed home. When Chris said, "Hello," all I could do was cry. I couldn't even speak. I cried. And cried. And cried.

"Babe, what's wrong?" he asked.

I went on a sobbing tirade about how it was the worst birthday ever, how I did so horribly, how they had me read stuff and that I had no idea what I was

43

reading. I told him I totally bombed the audition and they would never look at me for anything ever again.

I practically cried myself to sleep that night. I convinced myself that I was so bad that they'd never be interested in me. I got the WWF out of my head, so it wouldn't bother me so much.

It was my one big shot. And I blew it, big time.

On December 8, I flew back to Knoxville, miserable and hopeless. It took some time, but I eventually got myself out of the funk I was in, because I figured things couldn't get any worse.

I was wrong.

About a week, later we were working a shot in Morristown, Tennessee. Brian Lee and Chris were wrestling Tracy Smothers and Tony Anthony. Just as the match was about to start, I was getting out of the ring and standing on the apron, when Tracy suddenly decided to run the ropes, right in my direction. He hit the ropes where I was standing flat-backed, so I had nowhere to grab onto. As soon as he collided with me, I flew backwards towards the concrete floor at ringside.

The first thing they teach you in wrestling is when falling, don't put your hands down to break your fall. What did I do? I threw my hands behind me to break my fall. But instead, the only thing that was broken was my hand; my entire hand!

When I got up and looked at my mangled mess of a hand, I panicked and went into shock. I ran straight back to the locker room and sat down, hyperventilating. Jim came over to see what was wrong, and when he saw my hand he screamed. "Oh my God! Jiminy Crickets! What the hell happened?"

New Jack, of The Gangstas, saw the look on my face and somehow knew I was going into shock, which wouldn't be good. A person can easily slip into a coma if they pass out from shock. Chris ran back from the ring completely distressed, and Jim and New Jack told him to get back out there and finish the match, that they had me under control.

An ambulance arrived a short time later, because there was no way in hell I could have walked to a car to get to the hospital. As they carted me out on a stretcher, right through the fans, I heard them scream, "Tammy Fytch! We hope you die!!"

Oh my God! These people wanted me to die! How could they be so cruel? Here I was, mangled hand, severely hurt and scared, and they wanted me dead. The thought made me tear up a little, but then a silent satisfaction came over me—they hate me! They really, really hate me! I'm doing my job!

It feels very good inside when you try so hard to be a heel, and you generate enough heat with an audience that they want you dead.

So off to the hospital we went, sirens and lights and everything. After a set of X-rays, the doctor determined that I had five fractures and four dislocations. I had fingers pointing in every direction. It was literally too gross to look at. They set my fingers and casted me up. Hence, I sustained my very first wrestling injury—and it was a doozie!

Being the trooper that I was, I didn't miss a single show. I worked each night with my cast on. See, it COULD get worse!

About a week later, just before Christmas, my phone rang again.

"Tammy? It's Bruce Prichard from the WWF."

Oh my God! What in bloody hell could HE want?

"We looked over your audition tape and would like to know if you'd like to come up and start filming on Monday."

Now it was Friday, I was on Christmas break from school, so I immediately shouted, "Yes! Yes! Of course I would!"

Then reality hit. I had a fresh cast on my hand up to my elbow. I didn't exactly look as glamorous as I had on my last trip up to Stamford.

"Don't worry, we'll work around it," Prichard said. "Go out and buy some business suits and bring the receipt. We'll do what we have to do to hide your arm."

I hung up the phone and looked at Chris.

"Oh my God! I'm starting on Monday!"

But I still had no idea what I was actually starting, or what I was getting paid. I probably should have asked a few more questions. But we were overjoyed, and happiness was just pouring out of every pore. We spent the next two days shopping for the business suits I was told to buy.

I packed up Sunday night and prepared to get to the airport Monday morning. When I arrived in Stamford, I was picked up and brought back to the studio. I was then given the details of my new position.

I would be filming Monday, Tuesday, and Wednesday every week, and getting paid $500 per day, filming a segment for the televisions shows called the "Live Event News." I would be reading from the teleprompter (I hate that damn thing). My new name—Tamara Murphy.

It turned out that Vince loved my given first

46

name, but he wanted me to be Irish, like him, so he named me Murphy. (Coincidentally, one of his granddaughters is now named Murphy.)

Vince took an instant liking to me, and actually sat in on some of my filming. He took it upon himself to coach me in my delivery and inflection, and losing my accent. By this time I had my native New Jersey accent with a touch of Tennessee southern added to it. He needed me to be accent free, straight broadcaster style. He especially hated the way I said the word "garden" when referring to Madison Square Garden.

At first I thought he was picking on me a little, but I soon realized that if he was taking this much time out of his day, every day, he must have liked me and saw money in me. Vince McMahon doesn't personally coach just anyone.

So, this was the game plan: fly to Connecticut every Monday morning, film "Live Event News" for three days, fly back to Knoxville on Thursday morning, work house shows and TV for SMW Thursday through Sunday, fly back to Connecticut Monday morning.

But wait... where was there time for college?

There wasn't any time for college.

But for a 21-year-old kid from New Jersey making $1675 per week, every week, expenses paid, college really didn't seem to matter as much anymore. Beginning the spring semester of 1995, I was no longer a student at the University of Tennessee. Greed and gluttony had gotten ahold of me. Two of the seven deadly sins.

Irresistible.

I was now an employee of the World Wrestling

Federation, and that was all that mattered. But in a way, I kind of felt bad, and a little guilty. Here I am, not wanting to be in the wrestling business and wanting to be a doctor instead, and here is Chris—busting his ass every night because this is all he's ever wanted to do—and I get hired and make it to the big time first. But Chris didn't seem to care. He was genuinely thrilled for me. Besides, our money all went to the same place, anyway. If it bothered him at all, he never showed it.

So I went to work. I had my flight, rental car, and hotel and food paid for. All my clothes were paid for. I had a 24-hour passkey that gained me access to anywhere in Titan Towers or the studio. (I actually still have that passkey. I wonder if it still works?)

Every day after filming at around 11:00 p.m. (yes, I had very, very long days…in make-up at 7:00 a.m., out of the studio at 10:30 p.m.) I would go to the office building and hit the gym. At the same time, fellow studio employee Stan Lane (made famous in his days as "Sweet" Stan Lane of The Midnight Express) would also hit the gym. I had a feeling that Stan would have liked our relationship to progress beyond being just work-out partners. Stan would hit on me daily, and even though he was a very attractive man, he was about 16 or 18 years older than me. Plus, when he would be on the leg press machine and I got a good look at the top of his head, it was all too obvious that Stan's beautiful head of blond hair was… um… enhanced with surgically implanted hair plugs. Kind of a turn off for a 21-year-old.

Stan was very charming and very respectful though, and I did enjoy our time together in the gym.

These were valuable days for me, my studio days. They gave me a chance to get to know some of the boys who would come into the studio now and then to film something and to get more comfortable speaking to a camera instead of a live audience.

I'll never forget my first meeting with Owen Hart. It was early morning and I was headed upstairs to my dressing room, which was right around the corner from the make-up room. I opened the dressing room door (which was only ever used by me) and there was Owen getting changed—buck-naked with his pants around his knees about to pull them up! Ha! Thank God for him that his back was to me and not his front!

When he emerged from the dressing room, red from embarrassment, I sweetly apologized and introduced myself. We eventually became pretty good friends and spent a good amount of time together on the road.

CHAPTER 7
THE END OF AN ERA

While I was thoroughly enjoying my new line of work, the Smoky Mountain roster was expanding. This was a very valuable time for Chris and me—the SMW years—because of the vast array of talent we both got to work with and learn from.

We had the experience and wisdom of the Rock and Roll Express, Tracy Smothers, the Armstrong family, and the Heavenly Bodies. We got to work with legends like Kevin Sullivan and Sherri Martel. New talent was all around us, such as The Gangstas (New Jack and Mustafa Saed), Lance Storm, Chris Jericho, and Dr. Isaac Yankem, who went on to über-fame as Kane in the WWE.

Sherri Martel was very instrumental in my growth in SMW. She was brought in for a triple shot of shows to work ringside opposite me. When she arrived at the building for the first show, she wouldn't even look at me. I tried to introduce myself, but she wasn't having it.

I thought, "Geez, what did I do to make her not like me already?"

When it was time for our match, Jim explained

50

what we were supposed to do. She was only supposed to stalk me around the ring a few times and reach through the ropes and grab me by the hair until Brian Lee could come over and save me.

Well, stalk me she did. And when it came time for her to grab me by the hair, not only did she grab my hair, but she pulled me right up onto the ring apron by my hair. She then laid in four big, heavy forearms to my chest. She didn't work them, either; she laid them in!

When she was through beating the ever-loving shit out of me, she released me, the match ended, and I sold the beating all the way back up the long, long dressing room aisle in the Knoxville Coliseum. I coughed, I stumbled, I heaved, I cried—I had to make it look good.

Corny was waiting for me when I walked through the curtain.

"Oh my God, what was she doing?"

"I don't know," I said. "But I don't think she likes me very much. She almost killed me."

My chest was beaten red and already swelling, and I was stunned. When Sherri emerged through the curtain, my first thought was to hide under a chair, afraid that she might want to dish out some more punishment on me. We made eye contact and she bee-lined right for me. She grabbed me… and hugged me. Totally NOT what I expected.

"I knew you could handle it!" she said, squeezing me in a bear hug. "I had a feeling about you when we met."

What the fuck? It turns out that her beating me was a test of my heart and will. She beat the crap out

51

of me just to see if I could take it, handle it the right way, and not crumble.

Well, her test was successful, and from that day forward, we were sisters in the business. I earned her respect that night, and she always had mine.

And always will.

Sherri Martel passed away in 2007. She was a legend in her time and one of the business' premier women wrestlers. She also was inducted into the WWE Hall of Fame in 2006, shortly before her death.

Thank you, Sherri. You are greatly missed.

RIP 6/15/2007.

* * *

Chris Jericho and Chris and I always had a good relationship from Day One. We all had the same favorite band, KISS, although Jericho's idol was Paul Stanley and ours was Gene Simmons.

One night as we were leaving a show somewhere in Kentucky, Jericho asked us if he could follow us since I had a radar detector and he couldn't afford another speeding ticket. We said "sure" and I told him I would turn on the interior lights to signal to him if there was a cop around.

So we were headed towards Knoxville, and the highway ran through a set of tunnels that had been bored right through the mountains. There were no other cars on the road except for us most of the way, so we were flying.

As we made it through the last mountain, we noticed a silver bumper protruding ever-so-slightly from the dark shoulder, but the radar detector wasn't reading anything, so we plowed out of the tunnel at around 90 mph, with Jericho right on our tail. All of a sudden, lights and sirens pull out behind him, basically out of nowhere. That's when my radar detector started going berserk, but by then it was too late.

Jericho got pulled over, and he asked the cop why he hadn't pulled me over since I was driving the leading car.

"I would have," the cop replied. "But I couldn't catch them."

I WAS driving my Z-24, and I WAS a speed demon!

Chris got a ticket that night, and he still gives me grief about it to this day.

Soon Jim decided to bring in a childhood friend of Chris' named John Rechner to be Chris' partner and to become my newest protégé. Jim named him Boo Bradley. His character was a simpleton—almost mentally retarded—that I would lead around on a chain like a dog, and treat even worse. Boo didn't like to shower much in those days, so I was happy to stay a safe distance from him, like the length of a five foot heavy link chain, upwound when possible.

Our entrance music was "Magic Carpet Ride" by Steppenwolf, and his simpleton act soon proved effective, as he quickly became one of the fans' favorites. They loved him (because I guess they felt sympathy for him, or maybe they could relate to him) and hated me (for obvious reasons, but now even more so because of the harsh and inhumane ways I treated Boo).

We eventually started to use my cat, Buffy, in the story line. Buffy's name was changed to "Boots the

Cat" and she was my secret weapon to use with Boo, almost like his Kryptonite. When Boo would be losing a match, I would hold up Boots and threaten to do something terrible to her, and he would immediately gain the upper hand against his opponent.

Jim brought in the one-and-only Cactus Jack (who would become better known as Mankind and Mick Foley, *New York Times* bestselling author and three-time WWF Champion) to be Boo's mentor and persuade him to leave the "evil" Tammy Fytch and be a "good guy." Well, the combination of two simpletons as a team was more than the fans could as for; they were delighted!

So over the course of a few weeks, Mick was Boo's coach and corner man at ringside for a series of matches against Chris with me in Chris' corner. This was all leading up to the big show Christmas night in the Knoxville Coliseum, "Christmas Chaos."

The plan for the end of this match was for Chris and me to kill Boots the Cat.

Ok, we weren't REALLY going to kill her. This is what went down:

While Boo had the upper hand and was about to defeat Chris, I held Boots up in the air, stuffed her into a canvas bag, and threatened to toss her off a bridge into the river. Boo chased me down the aisle into the dressing room and then back out the other side. When I got back to ringside, I handed the canvas bag to Chris, who set it in the middle of the ring.

He climbed to the top turnbuckle and came crashing down with a big leg drop, on top of Boots the Cat.

There you go, we killed the cat.

What fans didn't see is the switch in the dressing room. Cornette was waiting there with an identical canvas bag stuffed with a small pillow. No one was the wiser. So what Chris actually dropped the leg on was the pillow, while Boots was safely tucked away in her per carrier in my locker room.

Voila! The old bait and switch! Works every time.

After the match fans were furious! They were incensed. They had just witnessed us kill a cat, and on Christmas Night! Oh my God, we must be Satanists!

Boo knelt in the ring, crying his eyes out, holding the bag in his arms like he just lost his best friend. This made him an even bigger babyface, which he remained right until the end of SMW.

Boo Bradley would later become Balls Mahoney of ECW and WWE fame.

By this time, Chris and I had run our course in SMW, and had already begun our journey for the WWF, as I'll get into in the next chapter.

As for Smoky Mountain Wrestling, an era was coming to an end. The last great wrestling territory could no longer survive on its own, and in a few months, the tapes and archives were sold to Vince McMahon and the WWE.

RIP, SMW. You were loved and admired by all.

CHAPTER 8
GIMME A C! C!

It was somewhere in the late spring of 1995 and I was told I was being pulled from my Live Event News duties and put ringside as a manager. Perfect! Soon after, Chris was given the call and was brought up as well. Naturally, it made sense to put us together at ringside since we had so much experience at it already.

We were brought into the office for a fitting for costumes and a meeting about our characters. We met with the Creative Department and went over designs. My outfit was a cheerleading skirt, a cape, a tank top, and gloves up to my elbows, and Chris' was a singlet and a cape. Our characters were supposed to be a cross between cheerleaders and superheroes—*ugh*. Babyfaces. Just what we both hated and despised being. We were natural heels. Couldn't they just stick with that? They had the costumes in mind but didn't have names for us yet.

We were invited to attend WrestleMania 12 in Hartford, Connecticut right after we signed our contracts. Even though we weren't officially on the road yet, we were still in production.

So we went to the show, and hung around at

Axxess and the PPV. This was the first time I was actually around real Hollywood and sports celebrities, and I have to admit, it was really, really cool.

And this show was *packed* with celebrities! There were Pamela Anderson, Jonathan Taylor Thomas (from *Home Improvement*), Tommy Lee, Jenny McCarthy, Lawrence Taylor (who would wrestle Bam Bam Bigelow in the main event), and a host of NFL Giants including Carl Banks and Ken Norton Jr.

Stars were everywhere.

At Axxess that afternoon, we met a nice guy named Paul. He told us he was just hired as well and he worked a little for WCW. He didn't know a soul at Axxess or in the WWF, and really, neither did we, except for the few I met while filming LEN, so the three of us kind of buddied up the whole day. A few times Paul looked like a lost puppy dog and I felt bad for him. At least I had Chris there with me, while Paul had no one. Paul just kind of followed us around a little trying to not get in anyone's way.

That didn't last long for Paul, as he soon became known as Hunter Hearst Helmsley and even better known as Triple-H. More about the name Triple-H later.

We had a blast that day and that night at the after-party. We got our real first taste of what the big time was all about and what was in store for us.

In the meantime, the powers that be had finally decided what we were to be called—Chris and Tammy, *Team Spirit*!

Chris and Tammy, Team Spirit? That was the best thing they could come up with? I had been a cheerleader throughout my teen years and a very good one at that, but Chris was clueless. And now they wanted me to teach him how to be a cheerleader and how to do stunts.

Now, Chris was a quick learner but I knew that he wouldn't be able to do partner stunts just by the mass of muscle he held on such a short frame. He just didn't have the range of motion or flexibility.

Our first live event and TV taping was somewhere in Western North Carolina. Wouldn't you know it—the town was just 90 miles away from where we slaughtered Boots the Cat! Great. And we were supposed to be babyfaces.

Half of the people in the arena were either there at the show on Christmas night and witnessed it live, or saw it on SMW TV that following week. Wonderful. We were just hoping they didn't recognize us… but recognize us, they did!

As soon as we got in sight of the fans, they knew who we were, instantly.

We got in the ring; I started my little cheer routine, and they started throwing things at us. There was *no way in hell* we were going to get these SMW-bred fans to cheer us. It wasn't going to happen.

As we returned to the locker room after a pitiful showing for our first night, we were met by Vince McMahon in the dressing room hallway. He stopped us dead in our tracks.

"Maybe you two would be better off as heels."

Ah. Thank God. Finally he saw it *our* way….Whew!

A couple weeks went by and we were in a meeting with VKM, Jim Ross, and Bruce Prichard. At that time, those were the big three in charge. As we made our way through some small talk with Jim and Bruce, Vince sat there with a grin from ear to ear just staring at me.

Finally, he stood and spoke up.

"I've got it," he announced. "You two are now heels. Your characters are a fitness-guru duo. Chris, I want you to be like Tony Little from the fitness infomercials, with his hype and energy. Your promos will sound just like his. We are going to call you the 'Body Donnas!' (This was a combination of body and prima donnas.) You are Skip and Tamara, you are now 'Sunny.'"

Skip and Sunny, the Body Donnas.

Chris' smile almost immediately turned to a scowl. Skip? What the hell kind of name is that? By the look on his face, I could tell he wasn't happy.

But, Sunny! My eyes lit up and my smile got bigger. I LOVED IT!!

What the name meant to me was sun... beach ... beauty... a bright, shining star. I couldn't have been happier.

But once again, I got the fruits of my labor and Chris was almost cursed with a terrible name.

Remember the movie *Twins* starring Arnold Schwarzenegger and Danny DeVito? Well, you can guess which one of us felt like Arnie at that moment.

CHAPTER 9
THE SUN IS RISING

Sunny was born.

This was my chance to take the ball and run with it. I knew exactly what I was capable of; now I just had to show everyone else. But I had a gut feeling that Vince already knew what I could do if I had the opportunity.

We were back in the creative department working on designs for outfits. Naturally, I had better ideas for them than the people in that department, so with a few tweaks and some sly insistence, I eventually got things done my way.

My first outfit was a sports bra-like tank top and bike shorts. A good idea, but not as tantalizing as I would have liked. What would a cute blond need to really catch the crowd's attention? I know. A short, flirty skirt.

So I eventually started to design and make my own outfits, complete with a smaller, sexier version of the sports bra and tennis skirts I picked up in sporting goods stores. I was designing and sewing Chris' tights as well. I got pretty good at it, if I do say so myself.

We were brought into the gym in the WWF

offices to film the first four weeks of introductory promo vignettes that would air on TV before our first match.

Vince was there again.

He began to explain how he wanted us to act and talk in the promos. He wanted me to be bitchy and conceited and Skip to be overzealous and extremely punctuated.

As he was instructing us on how to act, he thought it would be better if he showed us himself. So picture VKM, in a business suit, acting and talking like me—all feminine, cocky, and flirty. It was one of the most hysterical things I had ever seen! But here he was, again taking time out of his day to make sure I knew *exactly* what he wanted from me.

So we filmed four segments to air over the next four weeks, showing us working out and playing the part, each one more cocky, conceited, and annoying than the last.

And wouldn't ya know it? It got us heat.

When we were finally walking down the aisle to the ring for our first match, to our generic, nondescript theme music and Bertha Faye—like light show, we were heels. We were screamed and hollered at. And when I put the microphone to my mouth to cut a promo on our way to the ring, the fans yelled us at even more as they listened to my cocky rant of how they were all fat and out-of-shape disgusting excuses for human beings, while we were physical perfection.

Yep, we had instant heat, thank God!

We started out on the road with some easy wins over wrestlers such as Aldo Montoya, and eventually ended up in a program with Barry Horowitz. Barry had pretty much been a job guy his entire career, but a well-liked job guy. When he had his first match against Skip, the people actually got behind him and chanted his name, since they hated us so much. *We* were getting *him* over!

So Vince let Barry take the ball and run with it, a sort of "pat on the back" for doing jobs for all those years with no complaints.

All in all, it gave Barry a name. He got a T-shirt made for him because of it, and it proved that we were capable of taking someone the fans' hadn't cared much about and getting them over as big babyface.

They found a spot for us. We became mid-carders who worked with new babyfaces to get them over with the crowd. This was something Chris was very good at and actually rather enjoyed. He especially liked the fact that he was compared to "Pretty Boy" Doug Somers, a well-known heel from the 1980's who was a more well-rounded wrestler than most and did an excellent job of playing the heel and making less-talented babyfaces look like superstars.

Someone like that would always have a place in this business, and Chris knew it. There would always be a need for a good, solid heel that could take guys who struggled to get over on their own and help them get over with the fans.

Next in line was Louie Spicoli, a big-hearted 280-pounder from Los Angeles with surfer-boy blonde hair and the baby face of a 3-year-old, dimples and all. I used to tell him he reminded me of a cross between John Goodman and Chris Farley, which surprisingly he didn't appreciate. Our feud with Louie was fun. He was an extremely talented guy with a vast knowledge of his craft, and the agility in the ring of a 170-pound luchador. We had a blast with him on the road. He was scheduled to play a "Body Donna-in-training" and prove himself to us in order for him to be accepted as one of us.

Chris and I both became very good friends with Louie, and when we'd be working in Los Angeles, we'd stay a couple of extra days with him and do the town.

One day, we were driving around Hollywood on a sunny afternoon in my rented candy apple red Mustang convertible. As we approached the front entrance of Planet Hollywood, we noticed a huge crowd of fans and a sign for a movie premiere. Basically, these fans were all gathered there in hopes of catching a glimpse of some movie stars arriving at the premiere.

As we were crawling past them, we joked about how boring their lives must be, and just then Louie stood up in the backseat of the pony and yelled in their direction, "Go home and get a life, you bunch of marks!"

Just like that, a small riot erupted headed our way. This particular bunch of moviegoers did not appreciate what Louie was spewing at them, and angrily started advancing towards our car. We were all laughing hysterically as we drove away from them, until…

The traffic light turned red! We were now at a complete dead stop in the middle of Hollywood Boulevard, with an angry mob right on our tails.

Shit! Now what?

Just as the first fan reached our car and pounded

on the trunk, the light turned green and we made our escape. We probably laughed for an hour after that.

On another trip to LA, we were out driving again, this time on Oscar night. We decided to cruise around the after-party locations to see who we could catch a glimpse of (yes, we were doing the exact same thing that we had been making fun of those fans for doing).

As we cruised by the famed Spago Restaurant owned by world-renowned chef Wolfgang Puck, we spotted actor Randy Quaid (Cousin Eddie from *National Lampoon's Christmas Vacation*, amongst other films) leaving the after-party wearing his tuxedo, riding away on a bicycle! Yep, a bicycle-riding, tuxedo-wearing Quaid made our night.

You can definitely see some crazy things in Hollywood.

That angle eventually wrapped up with Skip and I not accepting Louie into the Body Donnas, though the BDs were soon to become a tag team.

During one match, Chris was getting his butt kicked really badly when the ref got knocked down. All of a sudden, a guy looking like Chris' twin popped out from under the ring and switched places with him to not only save Skip, but to gain the victory.

Same height, same weight, same body type, same wrestling trunks, all the way down to the same bleached blonde buzz cut.

After the three-count, I snatched the microphone away from the ring announcer.

"This is what true teamwork is all about," I gloated. "Here is *Skip* and *Zip*! The Body Donnas!"— or something to that effect.

Dr. Tom Prichard, formerly of USWA and one-half of the Heavenly Bodies in SMW (along with Jimmy Del Ray), was chosen to be that twin partner. What was funniest about his selection was that his brother, Bruce, who was in talent relations, begged to be the one to tell Tom about his new position. Tom was thrilled to be teaming with Chris, at first, because he and Chris always got along well since our Tennessee days, and they worked together even better. The funny part was when Bruce dropped the bomb on Tom that he had to cut his hair and bleach it blonde.

"Whoa, wait a minute. Cut my hair and bleach it blonde?" Tom exclaimed. "Hang on, that could break the deal."

You see, Tom was well known for his in-ring work, but even better known for his full head of brown hair with highlights, long and curly. Tom's flowing tresses would be the envy of any girl. It practically broke his heart when he thought of cutting off his luxurious locks, but hey—a job is a job, right? Making a paycheck is sometimes more important than your looks.

We were in Hershey, Pennsylvania, the night Tom had to debut, so we all went to a beauty salon nearby the arena to get Tom's hair just right, his brother Bruce in tow with video camera in hand to record the shearing for posterity and Prichard family get-togethers for years to come.

We walked into the salon and immediately the stylists starting fawning over his hair, saying, "Oh my God! Your hair is so gorgeous! What do you need done?"

Dr. Tom looked at them with an expression of disgust on his face. They weren't making it any easier. He pointed at Chris' head.

"I have to look like that!"

The entire salon erupted in laughter, and the buzzers and bleach came out.

This was a truly hilarious moment.

So the tag team of the Body Donnas was formed, and by this point my popularity was starting to rise. Well, the female fans still hated me, but the men? Well, they were starting to like me more and more with every flirtatious flip of my skirt.

At WrestleMania XXII, in 1996, the Body Donnas were scheduled for a match for the WWF tag team championship against the Godwins. The hog farmers were Henry O. Godwin (HOG) and Phineas I. Godwin (PIG). Phineas was none other than our old friend from the USWA, Tex Salinger.

At the end of the match, I was to jump up onto the apron and flash Phineas my cute little butt under my skirt. When I did, he was so distracted that he was rolled up by Skip for the three-count. We were the champs! And of course I took all the credit for it.

This was about the time when Vince started to notice my changing popularity.

And what came next changed the course of who "Sunny" was to become, forever.

CHAPTER 10
MOVE OVER PAMELA, THERE'S A NEW PIN-UP IN TOWN!

I was called into the office for a meeting and was told I was going to do my first bikini photo shoot.

Fantastic! I had only done a couple of bikini photos in the privacy of my apartment and shot by Kelly Cornette in my SMW days. I had never done a complete photo shoot. I was super excited.

We went to Miami Beach—me, the photographer Rich Freeda, and the crew; we hired a local girl for hair and makeup. We checked into our hotel, one of the classic art-deco hotels on South Beach. As we were checking in, we couldn't help but notice the fish bowl full of condoms on the front desk, and that the clientele lounging around the lobby chatting was all male. Turns out the hotel we selected was a gay hook-up hotel where most rooms were rented out by the hour!

We got into the room, and it was as seedy and as sleazy as we expected.

Umm, time for Sunny to check out.

I ended up at the Eden Roc Hotel, another art-deco type place, but this one was very upscale and classy… and very expensive. Perfect. Expensive was just my style.

So we organized my bikinis and cover-ups, chose the colors for my make up, and we were ready to shoot. My hair was done in a beach-blown sexy wave and my make up was dark, heavy, and sensual. I had dieted hard for two weeks leading up to this shoot so my body was lean and hard and toned. I was ready.

We shot photo after photo on the sand, in the ocean, skating in Rollerblades, holding a blue macaw—we took every opportunity that South Beach had to offer. We shot for three days and came out unscathed. Well, the crew did, anyway. I sustained multiple jellyfish stings on both ankles that were tended to by two very handsome, tan lifeguards. I don't know who was the lucky one, me or them!

We were finally finished and I anxiously awaited the development of the film. Yes, back in 1996 we used film. Digital cameras weren't around yet.

I had such an amazing time shooting and filming that I thought to myself, "I could get used to this!" My music video that the WWF released shortly afterwards was the footage filmed during this shoot.

I went to the office one day when the film had come back, and headed to the magazine department to check out the results.

I was in awe. Complete and utter astonishment.

My pictures were incredible! I felt as if I wasn't looking at myself, but instead looking at some model from the *Sports Illustrated* swimsuit issue. I couldn't believe my eyes. I never knew I had it in me to shoot photos like that.

I was given the chance to help choose what

photos would be used in *WWF RAW Magazine*. There were so many great shots to choose from that it was hard to narrow it down.

When the magazine finally hit newsstands, it was a smash hit. I only made a small corner of the cover, while Vader was the main photo. That didn't matter, though, because the fans were buying it for *my* layout!

At the same time as the release of the magazine, my new music video to the track of "Sunny" by Bobby Hebb was playing as I made my entrance to the ringside area. I couldn't help but turn around and watch the enormous TitanTron as my image, larger than life and in living color, flashed across the screen.

Almost overnight, my fan response grew from a third of the crowd cheering for me, to an overwhelming positive response from *all* of them! It was incredible! Do you see what showing a little skin can do?

Before long, I was 100% babyface, even though I was still managing heel tag teams. My magazine sales were through the roof, so Vince saw this as a golden opportunity and decided to make a T-shirt of me. He saw dollar signs, and he was right. My first T-shirt ever was a photo of me wearing a tight white button down top holding a pool cue seductively close to me, and the inscription on the shirt read, "I like it RAW."

It was an instant hit and a huge seller.

This gave Vince the idea of coming out with an entire line of merchandise with my face on it. More T-shirts, beach towels, pillows, CD-Roms, calendars, you name it.

Then it was time for a one-hour home video to be made. I went into the studio to film it, and not only did

I star in it and narrate it, I was allowed to help direct it and edit it, too.

Filming the narration was particularly entertaining. These were the days when they trusted you by giving you a microphone and letting you run with it, total ad-libbing. I was never given a script, not for ringside or for the studio. Vince trusted in my talent enough to let me do my own thing. He knew I had it in me to captivate an audience, whether live or taped, just by being me and speaking.

This is something that is completely unheard of today.

Even superstars like John Cena are given a script nowadays.

The video was a smash hit, and so were the sales of my merchandise. Within a short time, my royalty checks doubled my salary, but the WWF was making even more money on them.

I was pulled into a meeting at a TV taping one day and Vince informed me that I had just become the first celebrity in history to hit 1 million downloads of a single photo on America Online! I had soared past the likes of Pamela Anderson, Cindy Margolis, and the most recent Queen of Cyberspace: Teri Hatcher wrapped only in that Superman cape!

Oh my God! People were looking at my photo more than Pam Anderson's? I don't know about you, but I'd rather look at Pam than myself!

I didn't believe it, but it was true. It was even confirmed by America Online when they flew me out to Phoenix, Arizona, to be a presenter at their annual awards ceremony and introduced me as "the Number One most downloaded celebrity on AOL."

That was unreal. What was even more surreal was the amount of media my newly-found stardom had gotten me.

I was the first wrestling personality, besides the illustrious Hulk Hogan, to ever hit mainstream media. I was interviewed and featured on Hollywood gossip and news shows such as *Extra, Access Hollywood, Entertainment Tonight, Inside Edition*, and *MTV's Oddville* and *Singled Out*.

Soon after all this publicity, I got a phone call on one of my three days off from the road, that I needed to come into the office for an important meeting. I asked if we could discuss whatever we needed to over the phone, because I was only off for three days and then back on the road for a month. I was told that it was too important to be discussed over the phone. I needed to be done in person.

Great. I'm getting fired. That was my first thought. What could be so important that we couldn't discuss it on the phone?

So the next day, day two of my three days off, Chris and I drove up to Connecticut and walked into Vince's office. We sat down with Vince, JR, and Lisa Wolf, who was a higher-up in the office and sat in for meetings that touched on sensitive subjects.

Vince looked at me.

"We got a phone call," he said.

Uh-oh. What did I do? Who did I piss off?

"*Playboy* called. Their readers have been writing in, wanting to see Sunny from the WWF in their magazine," Vince said. "The people at *Playboy* didn't know who you were, so they called us. They loved the photos we sent them of you and want you to do a layout."

What? *Playboy* wants me? Were they serious?

He went on to describe that the photo shoot could be done either partially nude or fully nude, whichever was I was more comfortable with, and the pay would adjust accordingly.

Holy shit. *Playboy* wants little ol' me?

This was probably the highest compliment I had ever been given.

I could be enshrined in the pages of *Playboy* forever. I could be admired and drooled over (and I don't want to think about what else) by millions and millions of people across the globe, besides just wrestling fans. I could go down in history as the first female from the WWE to be featured on the cover and in the pages of the world's most highly acclaimed men's magazine.

It took me all of five minutes to say no.

I turned it down.

It was presented to me as a golden opportunity, but I said no. I just couldn't do it. I was only 23 years old and still very conservative about my body at that time, and I thought my father would roll over in his grave if I posed nude.

The look on Vince's face was of shock and a little disappointment, but he didn't try to push me or convince me to do it in any way. He understood where I was coming from and respected that. He always treated me like a daughter, and he probably wouldn't like his own daughter doing *Playboy*, either.

Vince treated me very well. I was his golden girl. In his eyes, I could do no wrong. And every time I flashed my million-dollar smile, the dollars just rolled in for him, and he knew that.

CHAPTER 11
SLOP, DROP, AND ROLL

While all this media frenzy was going on about me, I was still on the road managing tag teams. I turned on my beloved Body Donnas, much to the fans' delight, and began managing the Godwins, who just so happened to be the team to beat the BD's for the tag team belts. So I was *still* the manager of the tag team champs.

The fans were very happy about my slight babyface turn to manage the Godwins, but Hillbilly Jim wasn't too thrilled (he had been their manager up until that point). I got Phineas to fall in love with me, thereby becoming my pig farming puppet, but Hillbilly Jim knew I had something up my sleeve.

We went on for weeks, working shows where I acted like I was in love with Phineas, a totally dedicated girlfriend to this dumb hillbilly who wore his heart on his sleeve.

Finally, in a match defending the belts against the Smokin' Gunns, Phineas' love for me blew up in his face. I hopped up on the ring apron, sauntered sexily down the length of the ring towards Billy Gunn—the tall, blonde, good-looking one—and when I flirtatiously got close enough, he grabbed me around the waist, pulled me in tight, and laid the biggest, wettest, longest kiss anyone had ever seen in a wrestling ring—especially Phineas Godwin. He stood in the center of the ring and watched in disbelief, as his "girlfriend" betrayed his love by kissing another man.

Stunned, he was distracted long enough to get rolled up and pinned. 1-2-3, and the Smokin' Gunns were the tag team champs... with me as their new manager.

I was now the manager of three consecutive sets of tag team champions, another first in the history of the WWF. Take that, Captain Lou Albano!

Now I had to be a heel again, and although I tried my hardest, I still got the cheers, whistles, catcalls and "Sunny" chants due to the popularity of my bikini photos. Right after I screwed Phineas over, I had to go to the ring and give my "apology speech" to the world on live TV, and face-to-face to Phineas himself.

This might have been a challenge for some people. When Jim Ross walks up to you and says, "You have 7-8 minutes total. You know what to do," it kind of puts a little pressure on you. Again, no script was handed to me. They trusted me to do the right thing and trusted that I could pull it off.

I set off to the ring with JR. I started by telling the crowd how I knew how horrible I was towards Phin, how he didn't deserve to be treated like that, and how I wanted to apologize. Then I called him to the ring.

When he hesitantly got in, I coaxed him to join me in the center. He had a look of confusion and trepidation on his face, while I had a look of guilt, sorrow, and sadness.

I spent a few minutes explaining how sorry I was, how I was wrong to treat him like a mere possession, and that he deserved better. I told him that I cared about him deeply. Then I got him to say those three little words: "I love you."

I showed my happiness that we were "reconciling" our relationship and told him to close his eyes because I was going to give him a big kiss. He did, and after I shot the most vindictive, menacing face into the camera......

... *Wham!* I slapped him good!

Good and hard.

When the look of shock registered on his face, I began to berate him and call him every name in the book; well, every name that was allowed on live television, of course.

After about a minute of the trash talking, I called my trusted Gunns into the ring to deliver a beating to him.

I'm such a heel!

They did, even though they were late on their cue, and I hopped out of the ring. I was met at ringside by Hillbilly Jim. I turned and ran the other way only to bump into Henry Godwin. Apparently they weren't too pleased with me breaking Phinny's heart and slapping him across the mug. I turned and ran up the ring steps only to run into Phineas, who had made short work of Billy and Bart Gunn and now had his sights set on me. He was holding something in his hands...

Yep. The dreaded bucket of *pig slop*!

The Godwinns were well-known for dumping the pig slop over the heads of their opponents, but they couldn't possibly dump that on me, could they? Little ol' innocent me? A woman?

Phineas must have remembered his Southern manners, because he hesitated for a moment. I took advantage of his hesitation and began taunting him.

"He won't do anything," I purred into the camera, assuredly.

I was wrong. When I looked back in his direction, I felt the entire bucket of cold pig slop pouring over my head and down my body. I couldn't believe it!

The crowd couldn't believe it, either. They couldn't have been more ecstatic.

Even though I was technically a "tweener" at this point, they were still happy to see me humiliated and embarrassed by the slopping.

I made the most of it. I flailed around in the slop as I credited about it. This was my chance to exact a little revenge upon the fans that hated me for so long, so I took advantage of it. I grabbed handfuls of slop off the floor and flung it into the crowd.

Haha! The perfect revenge.

I made my way to the backstage area and got a standing ovation from the boys, not only for being slopped and taking it like a champ, but for the tremendous promo I cut before the deed was done. They knew I knew what I was doing.

I was then told that I would be slopped every night on the road for the next month. So much fun was in store for me!

What exactly was in the slop, you ask? Well, it was usually a combination of leftover salad from catering that afternoon, mixed in with some bread and water. I had heard stories in the past about the boys leaving the bucket in the guy's locker room all day for all the guys to ahem—urinate into, so I was careful. I told the road agents that I wouldn't get slopped unless I made the slop and I kept it in my locker room until it was time for our match.

A lot of people, even to this day, ask me how I could have enjoyed doing something so gross and disgusting. I truly did; I enjoyed every minute of it. Just look at all the publicity I got out of it! I was seen on every TV show, over and over again, replaying the infamous slopping, and I got a RAW magazine cover out of the deal!

Yay me!

I'm really proud of the fact that the WWF had so much trust in me, letting me adlib my own promos (that's what they were; totally off the top of my head). I'm also proud of the fact that they knew I could handle anything they threw at me—from birthday cake to pig slop.

Eventually the Gunns lost the tag team championship and I fired them. It was time for me to move onto bigger and better things... like my first singles champion.

CHAPTER 12
ALL HAIL, THE GLADIATOR!

Ron Simmons is one of the most famous African-American wrestlers of our time. A natural athlete, he excelled in college football for the Florida State Seminoles and then played in the NFL for the Cleveland Browns. As many NFLers do, when his football career ended he looked towards pro-wrestling as his new cash flow. When he debuted, there weren't many black performers making it big, but Bill Watts, promoter of the Mid-South territory during the 1980's, liked what he saw in him, and he saw dollar signs.

Watts had a great deal of success in promoting black wrestlers like Ernie Ladd and The Junkyard Dog, which is ironic because Watts had a reputation for being a bit racist. But he was impressed with Ron's athleticism and ability, and he made Ron a star, the first African-America World champion in NWA/WCW history in 1992.

Ron worked in many territories before settling into the NWA and WCW. He eventually became one half of the team Doom (along with Butch Reed), managed first by Woman (Nancy Sullivan) and later by Teddy Long.

Vince got hold of him in 1996. He couldn't wait to take this 285-pound monster and transform him into a top singles wrestler.

But instead of using his name value and his popularity to their advantage, the WWF renamed him Farooq, and made him dress like a gladiator in shades of turquoise, black, and silver, silly helmet and all.

Yeah, I know. It didn't make any sense to me, either.

Ron was talented in the ring, but was lacking in the interview department. So what do you do when a wrestler can't talk? You give him a manager as a mouthpiece.

Namely, me.

When they came to me with the idea, I thought it was a great opportunity. It was more exposure for me and helped me branch out into the singles division.

Then they explained to me that they wanted us to act like a "couple".

Yes, *that* kind of a couple.

Damn!

Now, I'm not racist in the least bit, but they wanted me to kiss him, tongue and all, on camera. I think that was the first time I think I ever said no to something they asked of me. Not only was I with Chris, but I just couldn't bring myself to kiss someone I wasn't attracted to, and I wasn't attracted to Ron in the least.

They respected my wishes and Farooq and I made our debut. Now it was a little conflicting, because here I am, selling merchandise like hotcakes as a babyface, and they want me to be a heel with Farooq.

Yet again, it didn't make sense.

So we went out, and did our best. Of course, I was cheered, but the fans knew that Farooq was Ron Simmons (whom they liked) and were confused whether they should cheer him, which they wanted to do, or whether they should boo him, which is what the WWF was trying to make them do.

Farooq plowed his way through opponent after opponent until we made it to the finals of the Intercontinental championship tournament against "Wildman" Marc Mero. This was one of the first times Marc introduced his wife, Rena, to the crowd as his valet. They called her Sable. Ugh. We'll get to her later.

When it was all said and done, Farooq lost the match, and the title, to Marc with a little help from a brick that was stashed in *my* purse—yes, my devious heelish plan had backfired.

After this loss, I explained to the fans through an interview that Farooq and I were no longer business partners, and I was going to focus on what *really* mattered: me! Sunny, herself!

CHAPTER 13
A HEARTBREAKING ROMANCE

Late in 1996, things started to get pretty rocky between Chris and me and we decided to take a little break. Many nights he stayed at his mother's house, or his father's house, or got a hotel room. When you're on the road with someone 24/7, you tend to get on each other's nerves.

We weren't totally broken up, but we weren't totally together, either. We kept up the charade of being a happy couple at work because it really wasn't anyone's business.

As I mentioned in one of the early chapters, I was in love with Shawn Michaels when I was 13 years old. So now, being a co-worker and in the same locker room as him, I couldn't help but admire him, up close and personal.

He was always very nice to me, much different from how he treated the boys—with the exception being the guys in "The Clique." He was extremely charming, and even more handsome and sexy than he was back when I was 13.

One night we had a skit to do together. He was going to be in the ring when a bunch of heels hit to take him out. He was to fight each one of them off and then call me into the ring. I was supposed to get in the ring like a shy schoolgirl, and he would motion to me to pucker up, like he was going to kiss me. He would then turn away and "diss me," as the live TV show went off the air. After we faded to black, he was to turn around, grab me, and kiss me, much to the crowd's delight.

Backstage, when everyone was talking over what they were going to do, Shawn pulled me aside and asked, "So, what kind of a kiss can I give you?"

Any kind of kiss you want," I replied, in the sexiest voice I could conjure up, giving him a little wink and a smile.

He was happy to hear that, smiled, and walked away.

So it was time. I'm ringside and he calls me into the ring. I walk over to him, he turns away, turns back and grabs me and dips me. He laid the hottest, sexiest, wettest kiss I had ever experienced, right there in the center of the ring. As he was kissing me, which felt like five minutes and was probably darn close to that, he laid me down on the canvas and *continued* to kiss me (and dry hump me a little as well.)

I gotta tell you—it was *good*... and I *loved* it! I didn't want it to end, and the crowd loved it more! They were howling like wolves, and I can bet you the women in the audience were wishing it was them.

It was a hot, hot kiss.

Call me crazy, but I felt sparks during that kiss. OK, I felt friggin' fireworks!

I mean, come on! It was the "Heartbreak Kid," for cryin' out loud! The most beautiful man I ever saw!

Ah, that kiss!

The next week on TV, I was standing by the curtain watching the show, as we all usually do, and Shawn walked up behind me to look and watch over my head. As he inched closer and closer to me, I could feel his hot breath warming the hairs on the back of my neck.

"Do you feel that?" he whispered.

The "that" he was referring to was his hard dick pressed firmly up against my ass. Oh yes, I felt it all right. Good and hard.

Instantly, I was turned on. I was moist. What red-blooded American girl wouldn't have been when the "Heartbreak Kid" pushes his erection up against you and gives you chills with his breath?

I had a pretty good idea where this was going, and what his intentions were. And I was right. Later that evening he pulled me into an empty locker room and kissed me. And felt me. And groped me. And then, like a kid in high school, he fucked me.

Yep, he banged me good, right there in the locker room.

It was so dirty and sexy and so not allowed within the crew that it made it even hotter.

Oh my God! It was mind-blowing sex!

And that was the beginning of the love affair that would eventually lead to my first broken heart—ever.

I was 23. He was 31. The age difference didn't matter. We got along like two peas in a pod. He was cocky, but so was I. We were both extremely attracted to each other and couldn't get enough of one another.

He actually said once, "It makes perfect sense for the top guy and top girl to be together."

I completely agreed.

We were all over each other. We had sex everywhere; anywhere and everywhere. Every show. In empty locker rooms, vacant bathrooms, broom closets, electrical closets, production trucks, and even in Vince's private locker room.

The only people who knew were the members of the Clique, and eventually Vince. Surprisingly, Vince actually approved!

He had a strict rule back then about members of the crew not getting involved romantically, but he approved of us. That became apparent to me at one particular TV taping, when Vince was behind Shawn and me in line for catering. He leaned in and asked, "So, how are *we* doing?" with a clear emphasis on the "*we*."

Okay, Vinnie Mac, your caught us, red-handed.

It wasn't uncommon for Shawn and me to go at it four times in one day at a TV taping, and a couple more times at night in our hotel. Members of the clique were designated to "watch the door" of whatever locker room we decided to occupy, usually Sean Waltman, the 1-2-3 Kid.

I was still on the road with Chris, keeping up the charade, so no one knew about Shawn and me, especially Chris. Even though we were just cohabitating, I didn't see any reason to upset him.

Once night after a TV taping in Syracuse, New York, I retired to my hotel room with Chris, and Shawn headed out to a bar with the rest of the boys. At about 2:30 am, there was a persistent knocking on the door to my room. It was Davey Boy Smith, the "British Bulldog."

"Tammy, come next door," Davey said, in his thick but sexy British accent. "Shawn got beat up."

Oh great. What happened?

I rounded the corner—Shawn's room was right next to mine—and I walked in. Shawn was a bloody, swollen mess. He had cuts all over his face, with the worst gash right below his right eye. His entire face and head was so swollen with lumps that he looked like the Elephant Man. What worried me the most was that he was bleeding from the inside of his left ear, and he was barely conscious.

Knowing that that could be potentially dangerous, I told Davey to call 911. I was worried about Shawn having suffered some inner ear damage or brain swelling. (I had been a pre-med student, ya know!)

So the bus came for him and I went with him to the hospital. Upon arrival, I removed his diamond earring so it wouldn't disappear, because they needed to do an MRI on his head.

The MRI came back clear, and Shawn came back sound asleep. He was either sleeping off all the alcohol he'd consumed that evening, or they'd doped him up enough at the hospital to not feel any pain.

When he opened his eyes a few hours later, the first thing he saw was my face. He looked a little shocked at first that I had stayed by his side the whole night, and then it felt like he had a "Nurse Nightingale" moment, and his eyes began to sparkle. It must have touched him that I cared enough to take care of him, because up until that point our relationship had been purely sexual and physical.

Then things began to change.

He was given a month off from work to go home,

rest and, recuperate. I called him daily, three times a day, to check on him. His mother, Ruth, went to stay with him in Ft. Worth to watch over him because he was getting bad dizzy spells daily.

Our phone conversations only brought us closer. We would spend hours on the phone sometimes, just getting to know each other better.

One day, during a nice talk about being on the road so much, I told him that I thought he needed a vacation.

"Yeah, I really do," he replied. "Where do you want to go?"

Me? Where do I want to go?

He told me to pick a destination, and he would book it.

"But what about my schedule? I'm on the road!"

"Don't worry honey, I'll take care of that," he said.

And take care of it, he did.

So I did a little research and found a resort called Ciboney in Ocho Rios, Jamaica. He had his ex-mother-in-law, who was a travel agent, make the reservations, and then he made a phone call to Vince to get me off the road.

Two weeks later, we were headed to Jamaica.

I told everyone, including my mother and Chris, that I was taking a spa vacation by myself—that I needed some "me" time.

I was scheduled to fly from Newark, he from Dallas, and we were meeting in Miami to connect to Montego Bay. I got to the airport, and I had a first class seat, naturally.

When I met him in the Miami airport, we were so

happy to see each other that we ran into each other's arms in the terminal, like something out of a romance novel. We boarded our plane, hand in hand, and the flight attendant brought him his Dewar's and soda, and me, my Diet Coke.

The entire flight, we couldn't keep our hands off each other... kissing, touching—we were tempted to find a blanket and do some more underneath the covers.

When we got to Jamaica, we boarded a small, old, rickety van to go to the resort. We were the only ones on board. We figured we'd take advantage of our first little bit of privacy—well, the driver was there, but hopefully not watching us—and I climbed onto his lap as he lowered my panties to my knees and I rode him as we rode the bus to the resort.

Yeah, we couldn't keep our hands off each other.

When we arrived at Ciboney, attendants in a golf cart greeted us and handed us mimosas. I still had never had a drink up until then, so he drank both. They drove us up the beautiful grassy hillside of the plantation, through all the fragrant banana and mango trees, to our room. Our suite, rather: a private honeymoon villa!

Yep, he had gone all the way and booked the largest honeymoon villa they offered. The place was gorgeous! It had three huge sections: the kitchen and living room area, separated by the open-air pool and Jacuzzi room, which led into the master bedroom, equipped with a king sized bed and bathroom, with a bidet. There was a bottle of champagne and a fruit basket on the dining table, with a card, which read, "Congratulations on your marriage."

Ha! They thought we were newlyweds!

We thought we'd have a little fun with it and actually pretend we were married. I moved the gold thumb ring I always wore to my left ring finger and we were now known as Mr. and Mrs. Michael Hickenbottom. We were invited to all of the newlywed functions and parties, and had a blast faking it.

We also had sex like honeymooners—lots and lots and lots of sex. Sex anywhere and everywhere. Privately and publically. (We were both mild exhibitionists.) In our private pool, our private Jacuzzi, in the public pool, in the ocean, on the beach under a blanket, against a tree on the plantation; sex was everywhere!

By the third day, we were both so sore that we had to take a break. We were having sex about ten times a day, all day, every day. Up until then, and even since then, Shawn was the best partner I have ever had.

He just knew what to do, and he was so sensual while he did it. We made love like champs. He did have this one small, strange fetish though. He liked to bend me over the bathroom counter and watch as he did me from behind, while I was applying ruby red lipstick, over and over again, just applying thick coats until I looked like the Joker from Batman. I never really understood what he got out of it, but it turned him on something fierce and got him rock hard.

Whatever he wanted, I did for him. Anything.

Dinner was even more special. Our personal chef cooked a private dinner in our suite every night, and we were serenaded by a guy with a guitar. This guy was great. He would play any request. Shawn loved

Elvis Presley, so each night he would request all Elvis, and when he would play "Welcome to my World," Shawn would hold my hand, look into my eyes, and sing to me.

He knew just when to be romantic. I would melt when he sang.

Each night after dinner, we would make our way to the piano bar, which was very mellow and laidback, but extremely fun. The pianist could play anything, and the entire bar would join in singing.

One night, when Shawn was ordering his regular Dewar's and soda, I told him I'd have one, too.

He looked at me, confused. "But you don't drink. Are you sure?"

I told him yes, and that one drink wouldn't kill me. After all, we were on the vacation of a lifetime.

So I had my first drink. Ever. At 23 years old. A Dewar's and soda. Shawn's drink. The Clique's drink. Vince's drink.

Just one drink. Then two. Then three.

Then I don't know how many.

I had a really good buzz, but I wasn't falling over myself drunk. The next morning, I felt fine. No hangover at all. I figured that since I didn't get crazy drunk, and I didn't get sick afterwards, that I might as well have more fun on the trip and keep drinking. What harm could it do, right? Wrong.

These few casual drinks on vacation at 23 years old were the beginning of the end for me, as you'll read later.

Our amazing vacation came to an end, and we grew closer over that week. We spent many late nights lying in bed talking, and we really started to bond.

At the end of our trip, we went back home, Shawn to Texas and me to New Jersey. I had to get back on the road, but Shawn still had another two weeks off. During those two weeks, construction was under way on his new home in San Antonio. He had shown me the blueprints of the house ... well, mansion is more appropriate than "house." He needed some help decorating and wanted a woman's touch in picking out the tiles and colors and cabinets and décor. His mom and I were more than happy to help.

She and I had become close, through our many phone conversations while she was taking care of him. We helped him choose different shades of Mexican tile for different rooms, the dark cherry cabinets and dark granite for the kitchen, and paint colors with a Southwestern flair.

A few weeks later, I was really going through a lot of stuff at home, and in my frustration I mentioned to Shawn that I wanted to get the hell out of there and move far away.

"Well, move to Texas," he said. "Move in with me into the new house."

Oh my God! Did Shawn just ask me to live with him? Was he serious? Was he joking?

I was so startled by his statement; I didn't know quite how to respond to it, so I didn't. I just giggled it off.

Finally, he came back on the road. I had really missed seeing him. He and I were booked on a tour of Canada together to do autograph signings at Wal-Marts, promoting the new line of merchandise the WWF released. It was just the two of us. This gave us some more much-needed alone time together.

It was during this trip when I broke down and said it.

Yep, I said it.

We were lying in bed just after more beautiful sex, and I told him, "I love you."

I really did. I meant it. I had fallen head over heels in love with him back in Jamaica, but was afraid to tell him. I didn't know what his reaction would be, or what he would say, if anything, so I held back. But this night, I couldn't hold back anymore.

I loved him. Very much.

He didn't speak a response, but he pulled me closer and kissed me.

Did he love me back? Did he? I desperately needed to know, but was too terrified to ask.

That tour ended and it was back to business as usual on the road.

Chris and I were on better terms now, and getting along well, and he moved back home with me. Shawn and I were still together on the road, but he did *not* like the fact that Chris and I were mending things. In fact, he hated Chris. He hated him because it seemed like no matter what, I couldn't break it off with him.

This was a huge hit to Shawn's ego, as he was very used to getting whatever, or whomever, he wanted. He didn't like that I went home with Chris after every tour. He didn't like that one bit. He was extremely jealous.

To tell you the truth, he was extremely jealous if I spoke to any of the guys on the crew too much... especially his arch-nemesis, Bret "The Hitman" Hart.

We'll talk about that rivalry in a little bit.

A few months passed, and Shawn's house was

finished. He didn't ask me to move in again, but he was still waiting for an answer from the first time he had asked the question. He's not the kind of guy who begs.

Shawn and I were in Las Vegas for the National Association of Television Producers and Executives convention. The WWF had a booth there every year. There were tons of celebrities everywhere, and we were the two top draws to the WWF booth.

One of the nights, after Shawn and I shared a beautiful dinner of filet mignon at the MGM Grand Hotel, we headed upstairs.

Then came "The Talk."

He sat me down and said he didn't think I had any intention of leaving Chris for good, and he was offended that I hadn't taken his offer to move to San Antonio seriously.

I began to cry. I knew where this was going.

I cried harder.

It didn't change his mind.

I cried buckets.

Right then and there, he broke my heart into a million pieces. I was shattered. I was truly and deeply in love with him, and he had just told me we were over.

How could this be? How could he just end it like that?

Well, a guy like Shawn did not take the backseat to anyone. No one. His ego was hit so hard, he wanted out. He wasn't going to be made to look like a fool in front of the boys if I chose Chris over him in the end.

My heart was broken, for the first time in my life.

About two months later, Shawn met a girl named

Rebecca, who ironically was a Nitro Girl for the rival WCW. One month later, she was pregnant. Another month later, they were married and living together in the house that I helped design.

They now have two beautiful children and have been together for 15 years.

I often wonder what life would have become if I HAD moved in with him.

Would I be his wife right now?

Would I have been the one to give him children?

I don't know.

Did he ever love me?

I don't know that either.

I hope he did. I really hope he did.

They don't call him "the Heartbreak Kid" for nothing.

You're probably wondering if Chris ever knew about the affair I had with Shawn. I can honestly say I don't know. He never once brought it up to me, never once questioned it. He never once asked me where I was for hours at night in a hotel, while he waited up for me in our room. He never once questioned who I went to Jamaica with. He never once accused me of anything.

Do I think he knew? Yes.

I mean, how could he not?

Then the questions remains, if he did know, why would he let it go on unnoticed and unaddressed?

My only theory is that he loved me so much that he chose to overlook it. I think the thought of living without me was too much for him to bear, so he let me do what I wanted to do, as long as he could keep me in his life.

I'm not saying this in an egotistical manner. I'm not saying I'm the best thing that ever came into his life. I'm saying that Chris and I were soul mates, true soul mates. And this was probably the reason I didn't leave him completely for Shawn. He was MY soul mate.

We were best friends. No one ever treated me the way Chris did. And maybe no one ever will. He worshipped the ground I walked on. There was nothing he wouldn't do for me.

So yeah, I think he knew, but the love he had for me was stronger than anything else in the world... stronger than any force of nature, stronger than life itself.

CHAPTER 14
THE "LOVE TRIANGLE"
AND THE MONTREAL SCREW JOB

I'm a very easy person to get along with. I get along better with men than I do with women, maybe because of how I was raised. Men find me easy to talk to and befriend; whether they'd like to get me in bed, or not.

Throughout 1996 and 1997, I found myself to be very close to two people—Shawn Michaels and Bret "The Hitman" Hart.

I was close with Shawn romantically. Bret and I were just good friends, believe it or not.

There was always a lot of animosity between the two of them. They were always battling for the top position in the company, always fighting each other for popularity with the fans.

I eventually made their hatred for each other even more intense, completely unintentionally.

Let's analyze this:

First we have Shawn Michaels—the arrogant, cocky, great-looking boy toy, known as much for his acrobatic ring style as he was for his handsome good looks and flowing dirty, blonde hair.

Shawn and I dated for about nine months. I saw a

side of him that no one else did, the generous, caring, loving side. Most people got the arrogant, cocky attitude that he displayed in public. Even though he could have anything, or anyone he wanted, he was also very insecure. His insecurity was sparked by his jealousy, and that is a recipe for disaster.

Bret Hart is a well-rounded performer who claims that he is "the best there is, the best there was, and the best there ever will be." He comes from a legendary wrestling family, with the patriarch being the late Stu Hart. They are famous worldwide, and legends in their hometown of Calgary, Alberta, Canada. Among those who know him, Bret is often called "The Lone Wolf," and that name absolutely fits his personality. Bret likes to keep to himself. He doesn't like to be around the boys. He likes his privacy. He's not the flamboyant personality that Shawn maintains behind the scenes.

For all of 1996, and some of 1997, I was the only girl on the road. I had my own locker room. In many of the venues we worked at that time, there would be a small backstage area, usually with only 2 locker rooms, one for me and one for all the boys.

Bret hated that, and he started using my locker room every night. There was no way he was squeezing into a room with 20 other guys. Wasn't happening.

So when I would change, he would leave. When he would change, I would leave. In between those times, if I wasn't off somewhere screwing Shawn, we had some really good conversations and became very good friends.

After that, when he would bring his family on the road, I became the Hart Family babysitter. Bret would drop his four kids—Jade, Dallas, Beans, and Blade—

off at my dressing room door. I quickly became well-liked by the entire Hart family—Stu, his wife Helen, and all 13 children and 42 grandchildren.

I was even taught the "Hart Family handshake" by Owen and Bret.

Shawn, whom I was dating, hated this. He didn't care about me babysitting the kids; he cared about how friendly his arch-nemesis Bret was towards me.

He cared about Bret changing in the same locker room as me, wondering what was going on when we were both in the same room. He cared about the jokes and the rumors going around the locker room about Bret and me.

Let's get one thing straight—*nothing* happened with Bret. We were just good friends.

OK... I take that back.

Something happened with Bret. Something *no one* knows about until now. I've never 'fessed up to in any interview.

Ever.

Bret did kiss me. Once. Only once. I didn't feel anything for him, only a very slight attraction, so the kiss went no further. Besides, I had too much respect for his family to disgrace them like that. I had intentions too, though. I did invite Bret to my hotel room once. He showed up, bright-eyed and bushy-tailed to my room. And he kissed me.

Sorry, that's all. I didn't mean to disappoint you.

Just a kiss. No sparks. Nothing more.

And this kiss didn't happen while I was with Shawn. We had already split up.

When Shawn and I broke up, his jealousy and suspicions actually got worse. He was convinced that if I wasn't sleeping with him, I must have been sleeping with someone else, and that someone else *had* to be Bret.

Oy!

At one particular RAW taping, I had finished up early and got permission to leave and get back to my hotel.

The next day at TV, the seamstresses and make-up girl ran up to me. "Did you hear what happened last night?"

I was clueless.

Apparently, Bret and Shawn had a face-to-face promo in the ring, and Shawn said, "So, I heard you've been having some Sunny days lately… " or something to that effect. The insinuation was clear. Of course, this infuriated Bret—which is exactly what Shawn intended to do. Bret's family always watched the show, and they liked me like me very well. Bret was livid.

Shawn was certain I had moved on from him to Bret, and wasn't going to let it go unnoticed or unknown.

I couldn't even understand why he would even care if something was happening or not. He was the one who broke up with me! It's not like I dumped him for someone else. It was all very childish.

Ugh, men.

Not long after, we had a PPV scheduled for Montreal, Quebec, Canada; Survivor Series, 1997.

The main event scheduled was Bret Hart defending the WWF World Heavyweight Championship against Shawn Michaels.

This what those promos were essentially leading up to.

Rumors had been swirling for weeks that Bret was going to leave the WWF for a while after this match, and maybe for good. Bret absolutely, 100 % refused to drop the belt that night for two reasons: 1) it would be to Shawn, whom he despised, and 2) it was in Canada, his homeland.

Vince told him that he respected that, and that Bret could "retire" as the champion, something that is virtually unheard of in professional wrestling.

Vince wasn't worried about the match. He knew Bret would put on a spectacular show with Shawn. Both of them always strove to be the best, and they would do everything in their power to put on an unforgettable match, even if they couldn't stand one another. What Vince *was* worried about was Bret "retiring" with the belt, and then showing up on WCW television with the belt saying that no on in the WWF could beat him for it.

Vince couldn't have that, no way, no how. That would be a huge victory for WCW in the Monday Night ratings war between the WWF and WCW.

So the dreaded night came, and we all made our way to Montreal. Everything was business as usual. Bret's family was there, his wife Julie, and all four kids. There were cameras there filming a documentary about Bret (which would be eventually be titled *Wrestling with Shadows*) and they were filming Bret throughout the day.

They filmed me chatting with his wife. You could hear me say that I couldn't believe he was leaving. They caught me on camera playing a game of cat and mouse with his youngest son, Blade.

When it was time for the main event, Shawn's

music hit and the place went crazy. He made his usual entrance, hips wiggling, strutting, and stripping off his chaps like an exotic dancer.

Then Bret's music hit and the place didn't go crazy: it came apart at the seams! This was their national hero and the fans simply roared. The sound was almost deafening. They really made it known who they wanted to win this one.

The match began. Bret and Shawn both battled like gladiators, each executing all of their signature moves. It was tremendous.

What happened at the end of the match has been the subject of intrigue, investigation, and speculation ever since. To this day, I don't think anyone really knows the truth—except Bret, Shawn, and Vince—and they're not telling.

Bret's patented finishing maneuver was the "Sharpshooter," a variation of the Boston Crab where your opponent is on his elbows and chest and his back is arched up, and his legs are under your arms. No one in the WWF used this submission hold except for Bret.

So when Shawn caught Bret in the Sharpshooter, every soul in that building knew it wasn't the end of the match. Nobody could *possibly* beat Bret with his own finisher, *especially* not Shawn.

So, Bret was in the hold, clawing at the mat, grimacing in pain, and trying to reach the ropes or figure a way out of it. The two men were in the hold for a minute or two. Then, all of a sudden, Referee Earl Hebner waves his hand in the air and signals for the timekeeper, Mark Yeaton, to ring the bell.

What? Ring the bell? The match was over? Bret submitted to his own finisher?

It couldn't be. It wouldn't be true.

Shawn let go of Bret's legs and turned around with a dazed and confused look on his face. Did Bret tap the mat and give up? Did Shawn just win the match and the belt?

Bret got up with an entirely different look on his face. It was a look of rage and confusion. And betrayal. And utter disbelief.

That wasn't the way the match was supposed to end. He wasn't supposed to lose the match and the belt that night. This wasn't what was agreed upon. He must have been double-crossed.

But by who? Shawn? Vince? The referee? All of them?

When Bret eventually left the ring, he stormed down the aisle like the Terminator, his eyes full of fury. He came into the backstage area, marched past me in the hallway where I was playing with Blade, headed right into Vince's locker room, and slammed the door behind him.

I was standing about five feet from Vince's door, so naturally I was trying to eavesdrop, but I couldn't hear much, only a few muffled voices.

About 30-seconds later, Bret stormed back out of the room, with his head down, grabbed his gear and his family and left the building.

Maybe a minute later, Vince emerged from the room with a blackened left eye. Right on his tail was Vince's son, Shane.

Oh my God! Bret just decked Vince and gave him a black eye for screwing him!

Or, did he?

Was it Vince who told the referee to make sure

Bret lost the belt that night? Did he tell him to call the match when Bret was in his own submission hold?

Or did the referee make a grave mistake by thinking he saw Bret's hand waving in submission, and not knowing if they changed the finish or not, went along with it and rang the bell?

What really happened?

No one knows, except those three people involved.

But there are a lot of people who have their own ideas about what happened, including me.

OK, here is my expert opinion as to what took place.

Bret and Vince always had a good working relationship. They always did well by each other. Bret definitely didn't want to do a clean job to Shawn that night, and Vince didn't want to argue about it. Vince sure didn't want to disgrace Bret by having him lose a clean match in his homeland of Canada. But Bret was leaving, and Vince needed that title off of him before he left.

I think all parties involved agreed that if Bret lost the belt due to some kind of "accident" or "screw finish" it wouldn't hurt his stature as a premiere champion because he wasn't losing cleanly.

So I think they agreed that when Bret was in his own finisher, the time when not a single person in that building would ever believe he'd give up and lose, if they had the referee call the match it would look like Bret got double-crossed.

And it did look like that. And Shawn played it off beautifully in the ring and backstage, acting like he had absolutely no idea what had happened.

This would definitely save face for Bret, and give Vince what he needed—a change of champions.

Why do I think this is what happened? Well, I'll tell you.

When Bret left Vince's locker room, I was standing right there. Vince emerged only a mere minute later with a black eye.

Now, I don't know if you've ever been punched in the eye before, but I have. It takes a little longer than a minute for an eye to blacken like that. It will swell right away, but the black coloring takes a little while for the blood to come to the surface.

Then we have my "forensic evidence." Yeah, that's what I'll call it.

I've done many autograph signings with Bret, and he is left-handed.

Now if someone is a lefty and they were punching someone in the face, wouldn't it naturally be the right eye that gets hit?

Left hand to right eye, right hand to left eye.

It would be uncommon for a lefty to throw a starting punch with his right hand.

Now onto our fifth person involved—Shane McMahon.

Vince's son was in the locker room with Vince the entire length of the match, long enough for him to punch his own father in the eye and give it 30-minutes to blacken up.

And when Vince and Shane came out into the hallway, they were both a little too calm for a scuffle to have just taken place a minute earlier.

Vince walked by me not even breathing hard.

Now, come on, if you just got hit in the face,

wouldn't your adrenaline be pumping a little bit? Wouldn't your face be red from your blood pressure rising?

Nope. Nada. Nothing. Not the slightest clue that anything had just taken place, except for that well-blackened eye.

So, after reading my deductive reasoning, do you think I should become a detective? Maybe, maybe not.

But it sure as hell makes some sense, doesn't it?

I sure think so.

It's been almost 20-years since that fateful night... maybe we'll never know.

CHAPTER 15
OH, WHAT A RUSH!

After Farooq and I parted ways, the company didn't really know what to do with me. They needed me, but they didn't really have anyone for me to manage.

We had a meeting, and they told me they wanted to put me on a production staff contract. I would now be working under Kevin Dunn, the head of the studio. My salary would be $100,000 per year. I would have an expense account (I wouldn't have to pay for *anything* on the road any more), first class airfare, and I would only be working nine or ten days a month, whether it was in the studio or on the road.

Fantastic! I'll take it!

I really was excited about the expense account and the nine or ten days a month. See, when you're on the road 300 days a year, paying your own expenses, you can easily spend 30 % of your income to live on the road, between hotels, rental cars, gas, tolls, food, and—of course—liquor.

Then, at the end of the year, you have to fork over 30 % to Uncle Sam. So a wrestler making $100,000 per year is really only taking home about $40,000.

I remember writing checks to the IRS for $30,000 each year, and it sucked big time.

So this deal was pretty peachy. They even let me expense my clothes!

This was when I started hosting TV shows. Almost all of them: *Superstars, Mania, Live Wire, Shotgun Saturday Night*. You name it, I hosted it.

Superstars and *Mania* were your run of the mill weekly re-cap shows, but *Live Wire* and *Shotgun* were entirely different. *Live Wire* was a Sunday morning show, live and completely off-the-cuff. It was an interactive show where fans could call in or email questions and speak to me, Todd Pettengill, Doc Hendrix, or any guest we might have at the time.

It was a pretty cool concept, but since we didn't know what was going to be said by whom, we had to be on our toes and quick thinking. There probably weren't too many others who could have hosted this show and pulled it off.

It was live, but we were on an eight-second delay, so if anyone said something they shouldn't or that was inappropriate, they could quickly edit it out.

Shotgun Saturday Night was a totally different animal. It was fun and scary and crazy and dangerous, all at the same time.

The shows were live, every Saturday Night at 11:00 p.m. Eastern Time. We didn't film them in a studio or an arena, but rather some very unconventional and sometimes uncomfortable places.

We filmed all across Manhattan, at the All-Star Café, Webster Hall, Penn Station, and a few nightclubs in town.

Webster Hall was particularly crazy. It was a nightclub that catered to the eccentric type of crowd. You had your usual clubbers, mixed in with some punk, Goth, and some of the NYC gay community. It was very normal to have a couple dozen cross-dressers and transgendered partiers roaming the floor.

They had go-go dancers (in tiny pieces of clothing, of course) dancing on pedestal-like platforms. Okay, correction, they were practically having sex with themselves on these pedestals.

We were getting ready to go on live in about ten minutes, so Vince (my co-host for *SSN*) told me to go out and pump up the crowd.

Okay, easy. That's what I do. Just hand me a microphone.

Nope, no microphone. They didn't want to bring down the music. He wanted me to go out and dance.

Dance? Me? Oh Lord, no. I couldn't dance! I had as much rhythm as a 90-year-old Chinese lady. There is no dancing queen here; hell, I didn't even know how to do the Macarena!

But, being the consummate professional, I went out, picked an empty pedestal, and started wiggling my ghetto booty.

Wouldn't you know it? They went crazy! I don't know why, because in no way was I dancing anywhere close to as appealing as the go-go girls, *and* I had a lot more clothing on than they did. But they were eating it up!

The one thing that stands out about the All-Star café was when I pulled Vince up onto our announce table and got him to dance with me.

It always amazed people how Vince never intimidated me, when mostly everybody else found him intimidating. I'd sit on his lap, kiss him on the cheek, and get him to dance with me on a regular basis.

Penn Station had to be the most fun of all the locations. The place was packed, wall-to-wall people. The show opened with a clip of the Undertaker acting as an engineer driving a train to the sound of Ozzy Osborne's "Crazy Train" playing in the background.

The TV Hollywood gossip show, *Entertainment Tonight*, was there that night to interview me, and to film me interviewing some of the fans. I grabbed my microphone and walked around ringside to find someone in the front row that I could get on camera.

Luckily, I came across a longtime dedicated fan and soon-to-be friend, Front Row Charlie.

I don't know Charlie's last name, but I called him Front Row Charlie because no matter what show he was at, no matter what venue, city, or state, Charlie was there in the front row every single time. To this day I still have no idea why. But Charlie was the perfect guy to interview—it made for a really good segment.

The energy throughout Penn Station was electrifying. It really was one of the best shows I hosted.

Unfortunately, *SSN* didn't last very long. Even though the shows were very good, the ratings were lackluster because it was hard to get viewers to tune in at 11:00 p.m. on a Saturday night.

When I was out on the road, I was primarily working the PPVs, TV, and doing autograph signings and PR appearances. My schedule was light and stress free. I was loving it.

I was being flown around the world to make public appearances. One that particularly stands out in my memory is my first-ever trip to London. There is a yearly parade honoring the Lord Mayor of London, aptly called the "Lord Mayor of London Parade." Imagine that.

Anyway, I had to stand on the featured float in the parade and wave to the Lord Mayor as we passed by his digs. I was also there to promote our upcoming PPV, "One Night Only," in Birmingham, England.

The studio instructed me to bring my video camera and go sightseeing and film it all. I was going to get paid to be a total tourist. Awesome!

I was roaming the city of London, alone, and soaking up all the culture I could through the lens of my camera. They made a nice little video montage of my trip for the TV shows when I got back called the "Sunny Cam." It was such a fun trip!

My expense account was equally fun. Everything was taken care of—first class air, hotel, rental car, food, gas, tolls, and clothes. When I was still working with the Smokin' Gunns, I told the office that I needed a few pairs of cowboy boots in different colors to go with different outfits. As Chris and I were walking through this one boot outlet in Texas, he came across a beautiful pair of $500 Stingray skin boots. They were gorgeous, and he had to have them. So I just charged them along with the six pairs I was getting. When I got the receipt, I noticed that it only said "boots," not "men's boots." So I sent in my receipt to get reimbursed, and wouldn't ya know it? They didn't even question it, and I got reimbursed for his boots, too! Ha!

Every time we were on a plane, there were only four people flying in first class—Bret Hart, Shawn Michaels, the Undertaker, and me. Not bad company, huh? The rest of the crew flew in coach.

We flew US Air a lot, and back then they used to send upgrade certificates for companions instead of having to redeem miles, which is what you do today.

Since I felt bad that Chris was in coach, I would upgrade him to first class. But then one flight I wanted to be generous, so I also upgraded Owen Hart, Bret's brother, and the Ringmaster (who later gained uber-fame as "Stone Cold" Steve Austin.)

Yes, even Stone Cold had to fly coach!

I continued to upgrade all three of them every flight I could, and everything was going smoothly until one flight attendant looked at me and the three of them around me in our cozy first class seats, with mimosas in hand, and said, "I'm sorry ma'am, but you are only allowed to upgrade one companion per flight."

I looked at her, and put on my "poor me" face.

"Oh, I didn't know," I said. "But they're all my boyfriends. You can't possibly make me choose between them!"

She looked at me with a confused, embarrassed look, and walked away. I had left her speechless.

After a time, Chris was no longer on the road, and was training the new kids in the training school along with Dr. Tom, and a few of the guys on the road caught on to my expense account deal. More and more of them started joining me at meals, knowing full well that I would pay the bill and send the receipt in to expense it. That worked for a few months until I got a phone call one day from Jim Ross, my immediate supervisor.

"Tammy, may I ask you what you're eating for breakfast for $90 every day?" he asked.

"J.R.," I responded, "You know how expensive it

110

is to eat healthy off a menu when you're maintaining a strict diet."

He just chuckled and continued cutting my checks anyway.

I used to get away with murder!

Steve Austin was just starting to gain his popularity as "Stone Cold," but he was still flying in coach. One day, during a flight, he learned that I had everything paid for, so he became my traveling partner for a few weeks. "Stone Cold" Steve Austin lived off of my expense account completely. He jumped in my car knowing that then he would get all his meals paid for, and wouldn't have to worry about gas or tolls, either.

He wasn't a stupid man.

After a couple of months, the powers that be found a new tag team for me to manage, and when they told me who it was, all I could think of was, "Oh....What a Rush!"

That's right, I was now going to be the manager of the one and only Legion of Doom.

The Road Warriors, Animal and Hawk, were one of the most well-known and popular, if not the most popular tag team in all of pro-wrestling. They dominated every company and territory they ever worked: the AWA in Minnesota, Mid-South, Florida, Portland, Japan, the NWA, WCW, and the WWF. Led by their brilliant manager "Precious" Paul Ellering, they were the only tag team to ever hold the tag team championship in every major federation where they competed. They faced the best of the best in the ring— the Steiner Brothers, Doom, the Rock and Roll Express, the Midnight Express, among others—and they beat every one of them.

111

Hawk was the more technically skilled wrestler, who also had talent on the microphone.

Animal was the powerhouse. He could press a 250-pound wrestler ten times over his head with ease.

Together, they were one of the most powerful and formidable forces to be reckoned with in all of professional wrestling.

Not only that, they were two of the nicest guys you could ever meet.

I was thrilled to be their new manager. Who wouldn't be? So I went to the WWF's head seamstress, Julie Youngberg, to design the perfect outfit.

Julie was the creative talent behind all of Shawn's fancy chaps with mirrors and chains and Bret's cool leather jackets. I knew she'd love to put her talents to work and come up with a female warrior's costume.

Julie did not disappoint. She dreamt up the wildest outfit, fitted to the skin, made of only molded leather and chains. It looked like something right out of the TV show *Xena, Warrior Princess*. It was to be red, black, and silver, and look like it was on fire.

Her drawing was nothing compared to the actual outfit when she made it. When I went for the final fitting at midnight the night before I was to debut with the LOD, my eyes widened with surprise and delight. It was the coolest, sexiest, most skin-baring outfits I had ever worn. It didn't cover more than a bikini, and my bare butt would flash through the strappy leather on my derriere as I walked. It didn't cover much at all.

So the night arrived when we were to make our first appearance, at WrestleMania XIV, March 29, 1998, in Boston, Massachusetts.

We waited anxiously at the top of the stage

behind the curtain as I helped them get fastened into their metal spiked shoulder pads and motorcycle helmets. All of a sudden, the house lights went dim, and the pyrotechnics on the stage began. The audio guys hit the magic button and the arena heard, "Oh, what a rush!"

The building erupted in frenzy. The Legion of Doom had arrived.

But what they didn't expect was for Sunny to be walking down the aisle with them.

They went even crazier!

I've got to tell you, the feeling that runs through your body when you hear that music *is* a rush! I've never experienced such a feeling just from a ring entrance. It was truly incredible.

The theory behind putting me with them was to make the fans look at them as a new tag team, not a couple of guys who have been around the block a few times. They thought I would bring youth and exuberance to the faction.

Although it was an honor to work with them, it was honestly a little boring. There really isn't a whole lot for a babyface manager to do at ringside except be a cheerleader, so I had to humble myself and get the spotlight on my boys.

Not easy to do with an ego like mine!

I started to travel with them on the road as well. Joe (Animal) and Mike (Hawk) rode with Steve Blackman regularly, so when I came along, they split for a more comfortable ride. I rode with Joe and we made Steve Blackman drive Mike around. Steve wasn't too happy. It wasn't because he didn't like Mike; we all loved Mike. It's just that Steve would have to be Mike's babysitter in addition to being his traveling partner.

Mike was one of the guys who liked to party. He loved his drink and he loved his drugs.

I never personally saw him do any kind of recreational drug, but I sure saw him take his fair share of prescription pill. Then again, we all did.

The hours-long drives with Joe were very valuable time for me. It gave us the chance to get to know each other in a way you normally wouldn't with a co-worker. We became great friends. We became family. To this day we remain that close. He has been my friend and brother for 16 years, and I love him for it.

Sadly, a few years later, we lost Mike to a heart attack, caused by overuse of substances throughout the years. Mike was a really good person—caring, considerate, and funny. He was well liked by all.

In 2011, alongside me, the WWE honored Mike and the Road Warriors by inducting them into the WWE Hall of Fame. They will go down in history as the greatest tag team that ever lived.

RIP, Michael James Hegstrand, 10-19-03.

You are missed by all.

CHAPTER 16
ARIBA! MEXICO!

Since I mentioned the use of prescription drugs amongst some—rather most—of the crew, I figured I'd stick this chapter here. There really isn't a place in my timeline about this topic because it spans over a few years, from 1997 to 2001.

Prescription pills were commonplace in the locker room, for all of the boys and myself as well. I can't remember exactly when I took my first pill, but it was shortly after I took my first drink with Shawn. And I honestly can't remember who gave me my first pill—either Shawn or Davey Boy Smith—but I do remember that that first pill was a Soma.

Somas are muscle relaxers. When taken according to doctor's orders, they affect the central nervous system and block pain to the muscular-skeletal system. When taken against doctors' orders, in quantity, they give you a really foggy high; they slur your speech; they make you stutter; they make you lose control of muscular movements when you walk. It feels and looks like your feet won't touch the floor. Eventually, you fall asleep.

The key to a good buzz is to take a few,

depending on your tolerance, on an empty stomach and eat something 15 minutes later. Within a few bites, you will be in la la land.

Somas were the pill of choice for us on the road. Of course we were using other pills as well—Vicodin, Percocet, Valium, Xanax, among others—but because somas are not a controlled substance or a narcotic, they were much easier to get. It wasn't uncommon for a wrestler to take 15 or 20 at one time. Your tolerance gets pretty high after prolonged use.

If I had to guess, I'd say there was maybe one person on the crew that didn't take some kind of pill. Everyone else was taking something.

On one of my trips to Los Angeles to go to some TV and movie auditions, I hooked up with my friend Louie Spicoli to take a drive down to Mexico. I had never been to Tijuana, so I wanted to go and do the touristy thing. Louie was a regular in Tijuana, and he told us how easy it was to buy pills there, and I'm not talking about a few pills here and there. I'm talking about pills in quantity. *Huge quantity.*

Louie and I took our three-hour drive south to Mexico. We went from pharmacy to pharmacy asking for what we needed—a bottle here, a bottle there—and it was all very time consuming.

It wasn't until I took my next trip alone that I found the secret to buying drugs in Tijuana.

I was walking around town, after I was bombarded by children trying to sell me gum and Pez, and I thought I'd stop for a break and a bottle of water. I spotted an outdoor café, so I sat down at the one table that had an umbrella to get some shade from the hot Mexican sun.

As soon as I sat down, a man walked over and sat down next to me with a pad and a pen in hand.

"What are you looking for?" he asked.

I assumed he meant what kind of drugs I needed, so I read him a list of pills and steroids and the quantities I wanted. He said "No problem," and disappeared up a staircase in an alleyway.

About 15 minutes later, he returned with a brown paper grocery bag in hand. He told me how much I owed him, which was ridiculously cheap considering everything I was buying, and I graciously paid him.

I was in awe. I couldn't believe how quick and easy that was. I got everything I needed in one stop! The bag contained:

1000 Vicodin

1000 Percocet

3000 Somas

2000 Xanax

2000 Valium

500 Rohypnol

Testosterone pre-loaded syringes

Vials of Winstol

And Clenbuterol tabs.

It was a pill-popper's dream! Why did I buy so much, you ask? Well, when the crew got wind of me taking a trip down to Tijuana, a few of them asked me to bring some things back for them.

Why not, right? What harm could it do?

With that quantity of pills, how did I possibly get them back across the border?

Here was my trick—and I don't recommend this to anyone.

Kids, do not try this at home.

I would go to Tijuana each month wearing a pair of overalls with a lot of pockets. I'd wear a baseball cap and bring a camera—I looked like a complete tourist. I'd go to a few shops and buy eight or ten Mexican blankets, a piñata, and a bottle of tequila with the worm in it.

The key is to park your car on the U.S. side, walk over a long bridge to cross the border, and walk back the same way.

Why?

Because if you drove across the border, there is a 99 % chance your car will be completely torn apart and searched when you cross back. When you walk, your bags go through a metal detector, but not your body.

So I would layer the plastic pill bottles between the Mexican blankets, and anything with metal—like the syringes and vials—I would put in the pockets of my overalls.

When you walk through security, they ask you what you need to declare. I acted like the happy tourist bringing blankets home for the family, and the tequila back for my Dad.

And voila! I was now a pro at the drug-trafficking game!

When you get away with that much, a feeling of exhilaration overtakes you, a complete rush of adrenaline. I was so proud of myself.

When I look back at it, maybe it wasn't the smartest thing for me to do. I did this once a month, every month for about two years. If I ever got caught, I'd *still* be in a Mexican prison to this day!

I trafficked copious amounts of drugs that were

worth a lot of money on the street in the States. Although I wasn't selling them for profit, I was still bringing them across the border illegally.

I would go back on the road and distribute the boys' orders, primarily members of the Clique.

At a show in Texas, I gave Sean Waltman a bottle of 90 Xanax, 2 milligrams each. By the end of the night, he had about 20 left in the bottle. How could he have taken that much and still be standing, albeit barely?

After that show, Chris and I got into our car and Shawn and Sean got into another car and followed us to the hotel. When we arrived, Shawn got out of the driver's seat cursing like a madman, his jeans soaking wet. Sometime during the hour-long drive, Sean Waltman had to go to the bathroom. Being so out of it from ingesting so many pills, he whipped out his willy right there in the front seat, and started urinating all over the dashboard... and all over Shawn! Ha!

Shawn was pissed off (pun fully intended) because he was supposed to wear those jeans the next day. Chris and Shawn carried Sean into the hotel with his arms around their shoulders and his toes dragging behind him. I was elected to drag in everyone's bags.

When we entered the lobby, the front desk clerk looked startled and asked if he should call 911. We told him no, everything was fine, that he had just gotten off a long light from Australia, and was jetlagged. Believe it or not, the clerk bought it.

I'm really happy I got over my pill-taking phase in 2003. A lot of my friends didn't get over it, and subsequently faced the consequences. I've lost countless friends and co-workers to pill overdoses, suicides, premature heart attacks, and car accidents due to intoxication. One very sad case led to a double homicide and a suicide.

It's really a shame to lose so many people in this industry to drugs. If only the WWE would have implemented its Wellness Policy ten years earlier, maybe some of those people might still be on this Earth with us.

CHAPTER 17
DIVA WARFARE

When I first went on the road with the WWF, the only other females in the locker room were Alundra Blaze, Bertha Faye, and Bull Nakano. Alundra (better known as Madusa Micelli) was the women's champion, and was only a wrestler; she didn't compete with me for any hosting, managing, or announcing spots.

When she left and took the women's championship with her to WCW, I was the only woman employed by the company for more than a year.

It was nice being the only girl for a while. I had my own locker room and I got all of the attention from the male fans.

And quite frankly, I'm an attention whore.

In 1996, Dustin Runnels, son of the legendary "American Dream" Dusty Rhodes, started in the company as "Goldust" and at his side was his lovely wife, Terri. Terri started in the business as a make-up artist for WCW and then garnered a TV role as "Alexandra York," the head of a group of wrestlers called the "York Foundation." Now she was Marlena, Goldust's manager and personal "director."

I knew who she was, obviously, so I welcomed

her with open arms. She was such a sweet person, with her Georgia southern hospitality, and we clicked right away. She would also bring their two year-old daughter, Dakota, on the road at times, and our locker room would become a giant playroom.

Terri and I got along great we would share curling irons, hair spray, etc., and never had a problem with one another. We were at a RAW taping in Hershey, Pennsylvania, and we decided to go to catering together after we set our bags down in our locker room.

In the room there were a couple chairs, and a folding table. We both opened up our gear bags on the table, and laid out our clothing for the night.

When we returned from lunch, we walked into our dressing room to find our clothes and bags on the floor and someone else's bags spread all over the table.

"Whose stuff is this?" I asked Terri. We were the only two girls on the crew!

A few minutes later, a woman we had never seen before walked in and sat down at the table, not even making the effort to introduce herself to us, a cardinal sin in a wrestling locker room, and just plain rude anywhere. Already I didn't like her.

"Um, who are you?" Terri asked the mystery woman.

"I'm Marc Mero's wife," she replied.

OK, but that still didn't explain why you are in our locker room and you're using our table. After some more interrogation by Terri, we found out she was going to be Marc Mero's new valet.

"So, what's your name," Terri asked.

"Rena," she said. "But I'll be known as Sable."

"Sable? Like the car?" I spurted out, without thinking.

The look on her face was priceless. "No," she said, in an arrogant and condescending voice. "Sable, as in dark or night."

OK. Whatever you say, Biatch!

So, right off the bat, she rubbed Terri and me the wrong way. But we figured that if we had to share a locker room with her, we might as well try and make nice.

Now, I'm not going to go on about Rena, frankly because she's really not worth the energy, but I wanted to put this in the book to clear something up.

I didn't like her. At all. No one did, really.

Over the years, a lot of people have speculated that I didn't like her because I had professional jealousy towards her.

That couldn't be further from the truth.

She had her place on the roster, and I had mine. I was the girl you wanted to bring home to mom and marry, the all-American girl next door. She was the one you wanted to take to a hotel room that had an hourly rate.

We didn't have the same character, just as Marlena was different from the both of us, so you couldn't compare us.

This is why I didn't like her.

She and Marc used to bring their eight year-old daughter, Mariah, on the road sometimes. She was a very quiet, but sweet girl. She had dark hair and a complexion like Marc, but I knew he wasn't her birth father. One day, while in the locker room with Rena and Terri, I asked Rena what happened to her daughter's real father.

"Oh, he died in a car accident when she was just a baby," she said.

"Oh my God! I'm so sorry to hear that," I said apologetically.

"No, it's fine," Rena said, as cold and emotionless as a serpent. "Him dying was the best thing that ever happened to me. If he never would have died, I never would have met Marc."

What? Oh my God! What?

Terri and I looked at each other at the same time. Did she just say what we thought she said? Did she just say that she's happy her husband and her baby-daddy died so she could meet and marry Marc?

Holy Shit! This woman had ice running through her veins!

She was the most cold-hearted, selfish bitch I had ever met. Terri and I were stunned. That was all we needed to hear. That solidified the fact that Rena was *not* to be liked.

But, again, we had to share a locker room with her. We tried to be as cordial as possible, which was much easier for the sweet and southern Terri than the cocky northerner that I am.

A little while later, Luna Vachon was brought in to work with Bam Bam Bigelow and the Oddities. Luna was extremely eccentric, to the point of being scary, and she wasn't the type of person you wanted to piss off. Luna was so tough she could beat up any woman, and most men for that matter.

Thank God Luna liked me. I affectionately dubbed her "Mama Luna" and we became fast friends.

One night at RAW, I had just finished at ringside, and I headed down the hallway to the locker room. As I opened the locker room door, Luna charged at me like a freight train, put two hands on my chest, and

124

launched me across the hallway into an equipment crate. She then climbed on top of me, and started pounding away on my head until all ten of her knuckles were bleeding. She then went back into the locker room, grabbed my huge Tumi suitcase and Halliburton briefcase and threw them on top of me.

I had absolutely no idea what was going on, other than that I was about to be murdered.

Our road agents came running down the hallway, pulled her off of me, and pushed me into one of the agents' offices.

Tony Garea and George Steele followed me in and asked what the hell had just happened.

"Your guess is as good as mine!"

What could have possibly made Luna flip out like that? What was going through her head? What was she thinking to attack me like that? What??

Actually, the question was "who?"

Sable.

About ten minutes later, the door to the office opened and in walked Luna.

"Oh Christ, here she comes again. Time for Round Two," I thought.

Instead, she walked in crying. Actually, sobbing. OK, she was hysterical as a baby who just lost her binky.

She walked over to me, hugged me tight and wouldn't let go as she apologized to me over and over again. The words were pouring out of her so quickly, and between deep sobs, that I couldn't understand most of what she was saying, until I caught her mumble the word "Sable."

Sable? Excuse me? What did she have to do with this?

Well, it turned out that Sable was behind the whole abomination. Apparently, she was jealous of me and knew that Luna would rip a Koala bear's head off if it were talking shit about her, so she told her that I was doing just that. Luna reacted just as she had hoped.

From that day on, none of the girls liked Rena.

Rena is also a compulsive liar, besides just being a troublemaker. To this day, she tried to convince everyone that will listen that she was the first one to be offered to pose in *Playboy*. She tells people that I'm a liar and that I was never offered the chance.

Well, the truth is, I was offered a *Playboy* spread a full year before she even started with the company, so how would she even know?

You see, that's what self-centered people do. They convince themselves of their own lies so others will believe them, too.

She also had everyone else convinced that she was only three years older than me, and three years younger than Terri. That would have made us 23, 26, and 29 years old respectively.

Well that was a lie as well. She is really six years older than me, the same age as Terri.

So now she's 46 and not aging well. When she appeared on a UFC broadcast with husband, Brock Lesnar, everyone thought she was his Mom! And now, since her daughter Mariah had a baby, she's a grandma… Ha!

And after I left the company, she made so many more enemies, that one of the boys (who will remain anonymous) took a poop in her gear bag.

Yes, karma is *definitely* a bitch.

126

CHAPTER 18
THE MOST ELECTRIFYING MAN IN THE WWF SCHOOL

1998 was an interesting year for me. Once again, I was doing double duty between two companies. Chris quit the WWF in 1997. He was miserable on the road. He felt like he wasn't working to his strengths and wasn't getting the push he deserved. In a fit of anger, he decided to walk up to Vince at a TV taping and tell him he wanted to leave the company.

"Well, Skip, you need to do that in writing," Vince replied, and walked away from him.

Chris, being the hothead that he could be, became even more furious. He walked up to Jim Cornette, who was now working for the company, ripped a sheet of paper out of Jim's notebook, and wrote:

"TO VINCE. I QUIT. CHRIS CANDIDO."

Yep, that's what he had the balls to write!

So Chris was off the road. This was about the time I started working in the studio on Mondays, Wednesdays, and Fridays hosting the TV shows, and Chris helped out Dr. Tom Prichard in the training school/studio warehouse, teaching a group of new guys that were under developmental contracts.

That group consisted of Olympic weightlifting champion Mark Henry, Sean Stasiak (the son of former WWF World champion Stan Stasiak), Sean Morley (who later became Val Venus), pro-bodybuilder Achim Albrecht (Brakkus), and a young, good-looking guy from a famous wrestling family named Dwayne Johnson.

Dwayne's maternal grandfather was "High Chief" Peter Maivia, and his father was none other than Rocky Johnson, who gained fame in the 1980's as the partner of "Mr. USA" Tony Atlas in the WWF.

Needless to say, it was natural for Dwayne to get into the business.

He was a very sweet guy, and very humble. You could tell he was raised right and taught to respect those who came before him.

Chris and Tom took a liking to him, and because of that, Dwayne received private training with both Tom and Chris. We could tell he had tremendous talent right off the bat, in the way he carried himself in the ring and the way he spoke.

On filming days, I would finish up around 5:00 p.m., and then go out to the ring in the warehouse and watch the training sessions for another hour or so until they were finished.

Afterwards, Chris and I would head down the street to this little pizza place that had a fabulous Italian menu in the back restaurant. One day, we asked Dwayne if he'd like to tag along for dinner and spend some time talking about our craft, because he was always eager to learn.

"Aww thanks guys, I really appreciate the offer, but honestly I can't afford it," he said, sheepishly.

"They only pay us $400 a week and I'm sharing an apartment with four other guys. But don't worry about me. I have some canned tuna fish at home."

Come on. A young guy who weighs 260 pounds of muscle cannot possibly survive on canned tuna fish. I offered to treat him to dinner. He gratefully accepted.

So there was the three of us—me, Chris and Dwayne—in the back of a pizza place ordering the best and the biggest dish they had on the menu the chicken montanara. It was this gigantic oval dish heaped with pasta, chicken, vegetables, and a creamy garlic sauce. And it was delish!

I could only finish half of mine. Chris ate most of it, but left a lot of pasta. But Dwayne ate every last drop. He scraped his plate clean!

He was so gracious and thankful when we fed him… it seemed like it had been quite some time since he had a filling meal like that.

What do you expect? The poor kid was broke! He ended up coming to dinner with us three days a week for a few months, on our tab. We were happy to help. He was a good kid and we enjoyed his company. Besides, we couldn't let him starve.

They finally started him on TV, and combined his father's and grandfather's names and called him Rocky Maivia. He was a babyface, but with the goofy outfit they put him in and his ridiculous Afro, the people farted on him.

They couldn't stand him and they frequently made their way to the bathrooms or concessions stands when it was time for his matches.

The office decided to give me the job of trying to get him over. They put me at the announce table at ringside to do color commentary for every one of his matches.

I basically had to try and convince the fans that he was the greatest thing since sliced bread. I had to convince the ladies that he was the hottest thing since Brad Pitt.

The problem was, when you try to force someone down the fans' throats like that, there's going to be a backlash, and Rocky felt the backlash full-force. The men hated that I was gushing over him so much and the women still weren't crazy about me so they despised any guy I liked.

So he bombed.

The office finally realized nothing was going to work and that Rocky was doomed as a babyface, so they made him a heel and put him with the Nation of Domination alongside my former protégé, Farooq. Farooq had ditched his gladiator togs and reinvented himself as the leader of a group of Islamic black militia types, and the fans hated them.

Rocky took over the Nation from Farooq, and then eventually became a babyface again, this time a huge fan favorite, with a new look and a new name.

He was now known as "The Rock," a name that will go down in WWE history..

He was a great guy and we were happy to have helped him. These days, he doesn't need *anyone* to buy him dinner! He has become a multi-millionaire and action-movie star extremely well-known around the world. He remains extremely humble and gracious to this day, and deserves every ounce of his success.

CHAPTER 19
MY EXTREME TRANSITION AND THE HYPNOTIST

By 1997, I was beginning to get frustrated with my position in the WWF. At that time, I was pretty much only being used as a model. They would hit my music, I'd walk down the stage and ramp wearing an Undertaker T-shirt and walk back.

That's it.

I was bored to death.

I argued with Creative many times asking, "If you have nothing productive for me to do, can I as least pump up my *own* T-shirt sales?"

There was a definitive no.

I was pretty aggravated about this, so I started accompanying Chris to ECW shows when I was off. Chris was now working for Extreme Championship Wrestling, which was owned and operated by Paul Heyman. Heyman had gained on-screen fame as Paul E. Dangerously a heel manager in WCW and the head of the "Dangerous Alliance."

He was just as good on promos as Jim Cornette, but with a New York flair to him. He also had a genius mind for booking, comparable to Cornette and Bill

Watts. He was a longtime friend and former roommate of my old friend "Hot Stuff" Eddie Gilbert, and he probably learned a lot of his booking ideas from him.

Since I was hanging out at many ECW events, Paul figured he'd try and get the WWF's permission to use me on a few shows. They obliged as a favor to him, and to let me have a little fun. After all, I wasn't doing much in the WWF.

I started making small appearances on some shows, going to the ring with Chris and the new faction he was now aligned with, consisting of "The Franchise" Shane Douglas, Bam Bam Bigelow, and the "Head Cheerleader" Francine. They were known as "The Triple Threat." I was having a blast. This was wrestling the way I liked it, and I was enjoying every second of it.

April 13, 1997, was a huge night for ECW. It was the night of *Barely Legal*, the company's first pay-per-view. ECW had built up a rabid fan base, but had nowhere near the financial resources of the WWF or WCW. Pay-per-view was the only way ECW could compete. But if that initial PPV flopped, it could have destroyed ECW. It was a huge gamble, and everything had to go off seamlessly.

The night of the event, Paul asked me to be a part of the production team and to help direct the show. My job was to sit at a monitor, with a headset and a stopwatch, to time out the matches and segments, give the audio guys their cues, cue the wrestlers for their entrances, and to tell the referee when to tell the wrestlers to "go home" and end the match.

This was a very important job because if the show wasn't timed out to a tee, we'd fade to black and go off the air with the main event still in the ring, which would have been an absolute disaster. Imagine all the buyers demanding refunds, or unsatisfied fans deciding to never again buy an ECW PPV.

The main event for that night featured the legend himself—hailing from the notorious Double Cross Ranch in Amarillo, Texas—Terry Funk. At 52 years old, Funk was a sentimental favorite; the godfather of hardcore wrestling making one final run at championship glory before riding off into the sunset. He was The Desperado, his pain and his hunger were driving him home.

Funk was facing The Sandman and Stevie Richards in a three-way match in the second-to-last match, with the winner of that match going on to face Raven for the ECW heavyweight title in the main event.

Funk has always been a part of my "wrestling family," and I have been affectionately calling him Uncle Terry since I was 17 years old. There was no way I was going to screw up the timing of his match.

So the PPV was underway, and everything was going smoothly. Nothing went overtime, everyone was right on cue. It was time for the three-way.

Funk, Sandman, and Richards delivered a wild, 20-minute show-stealing brawl, and to the fans' delight, Uncle Terry came out on top, earning the right to face Raven in the main event. The match started right away, and all eyes were on the ring... except backstage, where all eyes were on the clock.

The show had been timed-out to a tee, giving everyone enough time to shine on the PPV stage, but we were up against a hard deadline. Funk and Raven were going to war out in the ring. The crowd was rabid and cheering for Terry, wanting to see this historic night of extreme wrestling end on a feel-good note.

We were down to three minutes left of live airtime. I gave the cue to the referee over the headset to take it home. The cue was ignored.

I gave the cue a second time at 2:30 left, and it was ignored again. What was going on? Did the referee lose his earpiece? Are Terry and Tommy not hearing him?

Two minutes left and they were nowhere near the planned finish. I started getting louder yelling into my headset. "Take it home! Tell them to go home! There's only 60 seconds left until black!"

My pulse quickened, my heart was pounding, and my palms were sweaty. My blood was rushing through my veins. I just knew we were going to go overtime and fade to black before the match was over. And the fuck up would be all on my head. Unbelievable. The first time I'm given some real responsibility and control, I'm going to fuck it up.

45 seconds left; still going.

30 seconds left; still going.

15 seconds left and Terry finally beats Raven to win the match. Terry rolled out of the ring, leaned back into the fans at ringside. Five seconds left. He throws one arm up in the air in victory as he turns toward the hard camera... and we go off the air with a picture-perfect ending! The last 30 seconds couldn't have been timed better.

It was a miracle! I did it!

Paul was very happy with me that night, and shortly after that night, he asked Chris and me to join him for dinner at this great little Korean barbeque place in Manhattan.

Uh oh. Another dinner invitation to another BBQ restaurant by another owner/booker? Was this déjà vu, or what?

I didn't think this meeting had anything to do with me, but it did. Paul offered me a job. He would make me Chris' manager and part of the Triple Threat. He would pay me $20,000 more than I was being paid by the WWF. He promised to make a line of T-shirts for me, making me the first ECW girl with merchandise and to give me a higher percentage of the sales than the WWF gave me.

He also promised that I would have more creative control and more of an on-camera role than I had had in the past few months with the WWF. He told me I would continue to help produce the PPV's, which I *loved* to do.

How could I say no? He promised me everything I wanted. He convinced me that this would be so much better for me.

This why I call him the "Hypnotist."

Paul Heyman has a way of convincing people of anything. He could put dog shit on a platter and convince you it's a $250 plate of steak tartare

The problem with his offer was that I still had three years left on my new contract with the WWF. How would I get out of that without the noncompete clause taking effect?

Well, get fired. That was Paul's solution to that question. So a couple weeks later, after I made a WWF-approved appearance on another PPV, I grabbed the microphone after the Triple Threat's match and yelled:

135

"ECW is my new home!"

The place went wild! I'm sure the people at home watching did as well.

As for Vince McMahon watching at home, he wasn't too happy, obviously. The next morning, I had a fax from the office before I even woke up. It was my release.

Normally, people would be crushed receiving their release. Not me. I was ecstatic. With all the promises Paul had made me, how could I go wrong?

Well, I could.

The first two months were fine. T-shirts were made. Checks were given on time, and cleared at the bank.

Then Paul asked us to be the travel department as well. I would use the travel agency that the WWF used and book the entire crew's flights, charge them on my AMEX card, and get a reimbursement check once a month, for the entire monthly bill, approximately 30 grand each month.

All was really good for a few months. For a FEW MONTHS ... those are the key words. Out of nowhere, paychecks were late. Then our reimbursement checks were late. Really late, and the lag was growing each month.

One day Chris and I got a phone call from Paul. We were suspended.

"For what?" we asked.

Paul went on this tirade that he wanted us to go to rehab for our "pill problem" and enroll in some college courses.

Pill problem? College courses? What the fuck was he talking about?

First of all, the entire ECW locker room was on pills, and half of them were on some pretty hard recreational drugs as well, which Chris and I weren't. And there was NO WAY we had more of a pill problem than anyone else.

When we questioned him about it he said, "he loved us and cared about our futures."

Bullshit, he did.

Regardless, we were suspended without pay.

Then the mail came, and so did my AMEX bill. There was another $30,000 charged on our bill for airline tickets! But how could that be when we weren't working or making the reservations?

Well, it just so happens that Paul's assistant, Debbie, started making the flights in our absence, and telling the travel agency to continue charging them to the account on file, which had to be our personal account!

Son of a bitch! Those bastards were not only not paying us, but now running up our AMEX card and not reimbursing that!

After a few months, we owed American Express $175,000. Yep, you read that right. When we disputed the charges, we lost the claim because we had authorized charges for flights in the same names in the past, and had no proof we didn't authorize these new charges.

Un-fucking-believable.

So we were sitting home, in the new mini-mansion we had purchased a year earlier, paying the mortgage and bills out of our savings account.

That depleted fast. We had to work, bottom line.

We made a few phone calls and got word to the

WCW office that we were interested in coming there to work. We got a call from Kevin Nash, who was one of the bookers at the time. He said they wanted us and would call us back with a start date.

Great! We'd be working very soon. Fabulous.

We went to our first TV taping and an hour before Monday Nitro was about to start, they got a fax from Paul saying we were still under contract with ECW and could not work for WCW.

Fuck. He screwed us again.

Four more weeks went by of us going to Nitro, and a fax came through each and every time.

Bastard.

Finally, after a month of Paul not answering our calls, he picked up the phone.

We told him that if he cared about us at all, like he claimed to, he would either pay us what he owed us or give us our release so we could start working for WCW. He said he couldn't pay us because he was going bankrupt, but that he would give us our releases on one condition, and one condition only... that we sign off on the $175,000 AMEX bill and promise we wouldn't sue him for it.

What the fuck? Are you kidding me? The only way we could work for WCW was to swallow $175,000?

What were our options? There were no other options. It was either sign off on the debt, or not be able to work anywhere for another year.

So Paul's attorney/father drew up the papers, and we signed them. Reluctantly. We would now be liable for the $175K, but at least now we could work and make money.

American Express then proceeded to sue us! Our

bank accounts were depleted. All we had left was our new house.

This was my dream house, and we were forced to put it on the market.

I hated to sell that house. I picked out every color, every countertop, every tile, every cabinet, every fixture, every carpet. My dream home.

It was gorgeous. And soon it would be someone else's.

Luckily, the house sold within three weeks of listing, so we would be able to get rid of the debt quickly. When we bought the house, I wrote a personal check for $125,000. The price was $425,000.

We sold it for $525,000, but after the mortgage was paid off, AMEX got their money, and all the other credit cards that we owed money to were paid, we were left with just $35,000. I had spent $125,000 out of pocket, the house sold for $100,000 more than we paid for it, and after paying Heyman's bill, all we had left in the world was a lousy $35,000. But he cared about us and our futures.

Right.

Sure he did.

This is why I hate Paul Heyman. If he was to die tomorrow, I'd dance on his grave.

He definitely is on my list of the top two people I dislike a great deal.

Who is the other person on that list?

Read on, love.

I do have to admit, ECW wasn't all bad, though. The crew was a very tight-knit family that stuck together through thick and thin, and we did have some pretty good times on the road together.

Francine and I were always trying to see what kind of trouble we could get into.

On one trip to Ft. Lauderdale, we became crazy girls. We would always stay at the Marriot on the beach, and this one particular trip we were kicked out of the pool area.

Why?

Because I was carrying her around on my shoulders. Wearing bikinis. Thong bikinis. Not only are they prohibited in Florida, but from the back we looked like two naked chicks with only some strings covering us!

She and I would go shopping as much as possible to find new outfits to wear in the ring. This particular shopping spree had consequences, for me as well as Franny.

Chris, Shane Douglas, Franny and I were cruising around in the convertible when we came up on this lingerie shop that specialized in rubber clothing; ya know, bondage-style.

Well, the place was a little more hardcore than we expected, full of rubber masks, chains, whips, handcuffs... some pretty freaky stuff. I didn't find anything for me to wear, but Franny found this awesome red rubber dress that had a zipper all the way up the front and all the way up the back. It was pricey, $250, but she had to have it and it looked really good on her.

As we were checking out, the strange-looking guy working behind the counter looked us over. "Hey, there's a bondage party tonight at Tens," he said. We didn't know what "Tens" was, but he told us it was a nightclub on the main drag.

We decided to swing by the club that night to check it out, and we told the rest of the crew about it, too.

Franny and I retired to our hotel rooms to shower and get ready to go out while Chris and Shane grabbed some dinner. We got all gussied up, dressed to the nines. I was wearing a two-piece turquoise holographic outfit with a zipper down the top and on the pants, and Franny was wearing a floral print cat suit with flared sleeves and bell bottoms.

Ok, we looked like a couple of hookers! But how are you supposed to dress for a bondage party?

So we went to the club, only to find that it wasn't a nightclub... it was a strip club!

Oh well, we were already dressed and there, so we decided to go in.

When we entered, we saw that their idea of a bondage party was having the strippers all dress in S&M wear, and there was a torture rack in the middle of the floor.

There were men crawling around on the floor in rubber thongs and dog collars, being "walked" around by the strippers. Some bald guy, who obviously enjoyed being dominated, was strung up on the torture rack. His wrists, ankles and waist were strapped to a plane of wood shaped like an X and he was rotated so he was suspended in the air, parallel with the floor. He was being whipped and spanked by the strippers, and loving every minute of it. Freak!

We all started pounding back the drinks and pills, and even Francine—who normally didn't take anything—took a couple somas to get happy. Well, she got happy alright. I wouldn't say Franny gets belligerent when she drinks, but she definitely gets bossy and assertive. She had to go to the bathroom, but the only women's bathroom was in the strippers' tiny dressing room. She didn't care. She stormed to the back, right through the door, swung open the one bathroom stall door and literally yanked the stripper that was in there out by her arm. She then turned to the rest of them and said, "Get the fuck out. I want to piss in piece," or something to that effect.

They didn't mutter a word, and left. Franny wasn't someone you wanted to talk back to when she was drinking. She is the Queen of Extreme!

The DJ found out that half the club was filled with professional wrestlers, and he announced our presence over the sound system.

"We're loaded with some big, tough wrestlers tonight," he said. "If any of them had any balls, they'd get on the rack!"

None of the boys stood up, except for the one crazy one… me!

I've always been known to never turn down a dare, and if I could show up the guys in the process, even better.

Besides, I love attention.

So I strutted over to the torture rack, and let the girls strap me in. They tilted it forward until I was parallel with the floor. Then they proceeded to have their way with me. But they didn't beat me like the participant before me. Instead they tickled me with the cat o' nine tails and feathers and beads. I was laughing and turned on, all at the same time.

But since my arms were stretched out so wide, the zipper on my top kept sliding down. At one point, my boobs actually fell completely out of my top. Thank God the girls were considerate and kept trying to zip me back up.

All of a sudden, I saw a camera lens out of the corner of my eye. There was a photographer trying to photograph me on the rack! But before he could snap more than five pics, he got pie-faced and tossed across the room by Perry Saturn. Perry then threw him out of the front door, ripped the film out of the camera and smashed the camera to the ground. Turns out, he was from Playboy.com. Those pics would have been put on the website for all to see!

There was NO WAY the boys were going to let anyone disrespect me. So next, they all circled around me and the rack and turned their backs to me. They wanted me to have my fun, while respecting me at the same time, and not letting other patrons watch.

We always stuck together.

Another time, we were at our monthly show in Philadelphia. The arena was in an old warehouse that doubled as a bingo hall. Above it was a bar for the Mummers of Philly. The mummers were an association of locals, kind of like the Elks—basically a bunch of drunks who get together and drink cheap liquor.

Chris and I finished up with our match early, and because we had his little brother and two of his friends with us, we wanted to duck out early and grab some cheesesteaks from Tony Luke's. The parking situation always sucked there, so the boys would often double park each other's cars next to the side door. We walked out of the building to our black Sebring convertible, and started getting cursed at.

There were two drunken women and one drunken

guy yelling and cursing at us for blocking them in. They were Mummers from the bar upstairs

The woman who was yelling then threw her drink at me, and tried to throw a punch. The guy then threw a shot at Chris. I yelled to Chris' brother to go back inside and get Bam Bam and Shane. They came out and got into the action.

Meanwhile, the drunken woman ran upstairs to the Mummers club and came back down with about ten guys.

So it was ten on three, our guys were obviously outnumbered, and the Mummers were certain they had this fight won.

What happened next was a scene right out of an action movie, and couldn't have played out any better.

Sabu was "resting" in a lawn chair on the roof of the Winnebago that he used to drive around the country to shows. When he "came to" and realized there was a fight going on right next to his RV, he got up, took a few steps back, ran and dove off the roof on the RV onto about five or six Mummers.

Just as Sabu executed his RV plancha, the door to the building swung open and the entire ECW locker room emptied out onto the street!

Well, the ten drunken Mummers turned ghostly white when they realized they were now the outnumbered ones. Now it was about 30 versus ten, no competition at all. EVERYONE got into the action: Taz, Tommy Dreamer, Rob Van Dam, 2 Cold Scorpio, the FBI, the Dudleys … everyone.

It was a massive street fight which was eventually watched and cheered on by some fans that were alerted and rushed out the front door.

The funniest moment of the entire fight, besides Sabu's death defying dive, was when "Wild Fire" Tommy Rich got involved. Tommy is a former NWA heavyweight champion, but after years of drug abuse and alcoholism, he isn't quite the same mentally as he once was.

So instead of coming out like a ball of fire, swinging, he naturally grabbed a Mummer, put him in a headlock, and took him over onto the ground, like he was in a wrestling match! Then he just lay there, on the ground, with the guy's head still in his arms! He was probably shouting at the guy to sell!

Francine's red rubber dress came into play on another show in Philly. This episode ended badly for Franny, but extremely well for the fans.

We had just started an angle where Bam Bam would turn on the Triple Threat. After Bam Bam cleared the ring of Shane and Chris, he grabbed me and set me on his shoulder to deliver his "Greetings from Asbury Park" finisher, which was a variation of a power slam. After he hoisted me up, Francine made her way down the aisle to make the save. As she lifted her knee to the ring apron, the back zipper of the rubber dress completely popped open, revealing her bare back and bare butt cheeks with the slight glimpse of a thong between them.

But hey, she's hardcore, so that didn't stop her.

As she climbed through the ropes to get into the ring, low and behold, the FRONT zipper completely popped open!

Now she was in the ring, with only a tiny thong and a wide-open rubber dress hanging off of her shoulders—

Braless!

But hey, she's a pro, so even that didn't stop her!

She ran over to Bam Bam, who then hoisted HER up onto his other shoulder.

Both of us in the air on his shoulders, we were supposed to be scared and screaming for our lives, about to meet our fate at the hands of the "Beast from the East." But instead of crying in fear, all I could do was laugh my ass off hysterically at the sight of a naked Francine, laughing at herself as well.

Well, this was one moment in ECW history that was photographed a thousand times.

Ah… the memories!

I guess with the exception of my lost $175K, the good in ECW outweighed the bad. I, as well as most fans out there, wish it was still around. Those were some of the best live shows I had ever witnessed and I'd love to do it over again.

Just not with Paul Heyman as a boss.

CHAPTER 20
HEAVEN NEEDED AN ANGEL

In the spring of 1997, while I was still working my light schedule and Chris was already on the road for ECW, I was home for a few days and staying at my mother's house in New Jersey while Chris was in Poughkeepsie, New York.

It was May. Still very cold at night, but a hint of spring would arrive when the sun rose each day. Spring skiing was coming to an end, and I had just taken my niece, Stacey, skiing a few weeks earlier.

My sister, Lori, gave birth to Stacey Noreen on December 15, 1980; I was just eight years old. Because we were so close in age, we didn't have a typical aunt/niece relationship. We were more like sisters.

Stacey was beautiful. She had an innocent face, fair skin, straight, silky blonde hair, and blue eyes. This kid could do anything. She was extremely talented and way too smart for her own good. She was intelligent, a straight A student. She could act, sing, and she was funny as hell. Whether she told a joke or contorted her face some crazy way, you couldn't help but laugh with her.

147

She was also a natural athlete. When she was eight years old, I took her skiing for the first time. She was bored to death in the beginner's class and begged me to just let her hit the slopes. Reluctantly, I agreed.

We got to the top of the mountain and, remarkably, she went soaring down the slope, dropping her poles in her wake. I couldn't believe it! Was there *anything* she couldn't do? After that jaw-dropping day, we continued to go skiing together as much as possible, every weekend if we could.

As she got into her teens, we became even closer. I was her big sister, her Aunt Tammy, her second mother. She would come to me with teenage issues that she didn't feel comfortable discussing with her mom.

I was her ear, her therapist, when she was mad at her parents or friends. I had planned to buy her very first car, a Jeep, when she turned 16, and she wanted to come and live with Chris and me when she turned 18.

My mom and I were sound asleep at 2:00 a.m. when I heard the phone ring in the kitchen. I jumped out of bed and picked up the receiver.

It was my sister, Lori.

She said that Stacey was in a bad car accident and was going into surgery, and it didn't look good. She said we should get up to Pennsylvania right away.

It didn't look good? Surgery? What was going on? She didn't go into any details.

I woke my Mom up and we got dressed. I called Chris next and told him to meet me at the hospital. I was about two hours away and he was three hours away. He said he was leaving Poughkeepsie immediately and would get there as soon as possible.

My mom and I rushed to the hospital and arrived around 4:30 a.m. Stacey had already gone through surgery twice. She lay there in a hospital bed with her head shaved and wrapped in bandages, on life support.

With the exception of the white bandages, she looked unharmed. Not a scratch or bruise on her face. No broken bones. The only blood was a slow trickle coming out of her right ear.

She looked like an angel sleeping.

What happened? And what was wrong with her?

She was headed home from her boyfriend's house. Her curfew was 11:00 p.m., and she was never late. She had just gotten her driver's license less than six months earlier. At 11:20 p.m., her father started getting worried. Something was wrong. He headed out in the car down the road, headed towards her boyfriend's house. After about only a mile on the road, he saw a group of flashing lights up around the next bend.

His heart sunk into his stomach. He just knew it had to be for her.

As he approached, a lump formed in his throat when he saw a Nissan Altima up against a tree on someone's front lawn.

It was Lori's car.

The police and EMT's told him that she lost control of the car, skidded off the road, and hit the tree head-on. She hit her head on the windshield and was unconscious when they arrived.

She wasn't wearing her seatbelt.

The paramedics airlifted her to the hospital in Allentown, Pennsylvania, and they called a team of neurosurgeons in for her.

She had no cuts. No bruises. No blood. But her brain was swelling at a rapid rate.

They needed to go in and remove a part of her skull to hopefully relieve pressure and stop the brain from swelling even more.

The first surgery didn't work. They had to do a second surgery.

That didn't work either.

The head surgeon came into the room and said that Stacey's had only about five percent of her brain function remaining. If she ever woke up, she would be mentally handicapped for life.

Oh my God.

Why Stacey? Why her?

She had everything in the world going for her— everything.

She was our angel... My only niece.

My little sister.

My daughter.

My best friend.

It was almost 9:00 a.m. when my sister and her husband decided to take their sweet baby girl off life support. Less than 15 minutes later, her heart came to a stop.

I was holding her hand when it did.

She was just 16 years old.

It was my second major traumatic experience, and my second loss, after my father.

I was crushed. I couldn't imagine life without her. This was when my drinking and pill taking increased to monumental levels.

She was my little girl. I loved her as much as I loved Chris, and he loved her just as much as I did.

Even though I don't have her in my life anymore, I will always have our memories.

Chris, my mom, Stacey and I took a trip to Florida about a year before she died. We had so much fun. She was such a little prankster, too. One night, Chris and I were downstairs in the hotel Jacuzzi when Stacey came down with a devious look on her face. She emptied an entire bottle of shampoo into the tub, and the patio surrounding it soon looked like it had been hit by a blizzard.

One night, at sunset, she wanted to take a walk on the beach, but we didn't want her to go alone. So Chris said he'd walk with her. She was cool with that because she really loved him. As they were walking past an elderly couple taking in the beautiful sky, she grabbed his hand, started pulling on his arm as if to try and get away, and started yelling, "Pedophile! Pedophile! Help me! Pedophile!"

Chris immediately got red and sweaty from embarrassment, thinking the couple was going to call the authorities and report a pedophile on Clearwater Beach!

Like I said, she was too smart and witty and funny for her own good.

I love you and miss you, kiddo.

The world is just not the same without you in it.

RIP Stacey Noreen Cotton, 5-17-97.

Our angel.

CHAPTER 21
WCW-THE COMPANY FROM HELL

In late 1999, after our releases from ECW were finally granted, we began working for WCW.

We were not only excited to be working and getting paid again, but we were anxious to share a locker room with some of the most well-known performers in the business, most notably the "Nature Boy" Ric Flair.

Flair was the one person that Chris always dreamed of wrestling, and I had always dreamed of managing. Chris would get his wish. I, unfortunately, wouldn't.

We entered WCW with high hopes of restoring our slightly tarnished careers to where they once were., but WCW proved very quickly that they did not know how to utilize the talent they had under contract.

For example, I was the manager of champions. My strengths are my microphone skills and crowd appeal. Instead of using those skills, they had me wrestling in mixed tag team matches the entire time I was there.

Chris and I either wrestled the teams of Crowbar and Daffney or Prince Iaukea and Paisley. One Nitro I even had a singles match against Mona (who later became Molly Holly).

Now, I ask you: Would you put a girl who wasn't a wrestler, never had any experience as a wrestler, and who openly admitted that she wasn't any good at it, in wrestling matches?

This is what I mean when I say that nothing WCW did made any sense. It was rather surprising too, because the booker was Vince Russo, and he knew my strengths from working with me in the WWF. But then again, with the WWF, Vince Russo was only the editor of *RAW Magazine.* WCW decided it would be a good idea to give him all the creative control over every wrestler, match, and angle in the company.

Great idea, right? Wrong! Way wrong. Couldn't be more wrong.

Vince Russo, under the guidance of Eric Bischoff, proceeded to run WCW into the ground. They put two people with absolutely no knowledge of how to book a wrestling company in charge of booking a wrestling company! Stupid.

For a while, WCW looked promising. Throughout the famed "Monday Night Wars" between the WWF's RAW and WCW's Nitro, both companies pushed each other creatively, and weekly ratings (and quarterly ratings) were analyzed ad infinitum. WCW consistently beat the WWF in the Monday night ratings for about two years straight, before the WWF eventually surpassed them during the height of the popularity of "Stone Cold" Steve Austin and "The Attitude Era." But WCW's early dominance wasn't because it had better angles or matches or wrestlers, or an overall better product.

It was because they gave it all away for free.

You know that old saying, "why buy the cow when you can get the milk for free?" That's exactly what happened.

What do I mean?

Well, the key to having a financially successful wrestling company is to give just enough product for free on TV to tease and spark enough interest for fans to go out and pay $40, $50, $100 per ticket to see what happens live.

Wrestling is a soap opera. All the angles, matches, interviews, sneak attacks and dastardly things wrestlers do are meant to make you want to watch your favorites beat your most hated to a pulp, once and for all.

After watching all of this build up on TV, it should make you absolutely, no doubt about it, shell out that hard-earned money to see it the payoff matches, either live or on pay-per-view.

WCW had a twisted vision. Bischoff and Russo were all about ratings. They wholeheartedly believed that if they beat the WWF in the Monday Night television ratings, they would be declared the superior wrestling organization.

So what did they do?

They put the culmination and climax of all their angles on *free* live TV! They gave it all away! That's why their ratings were up. Why buy the cow when you can get the milk for free, right?

Come time to sell tickets, no one was interested. They had already seen it all.

While the WWF was consistently selling out arenas, WCW was drawing maybe a quarter of an arena's worth of fans.

I was in shock when I worked my first WCW show. I couldn't believe they were only filling 5,000 seats in 20,000 seat arenas!

I mean, couldn't someone just grab the two of them and shake some sense into them? Couldn't someone tell Ted Turner, the company's owner, that Russo and Bischoff were killing the company?

The thing was, no one wanted to. No one cared. The entire locker room was disgruntled and complacent. Because of that disinterest, they were just happy to get their paychecks and go home.

They had seen the company being run into the ground and their talents being wasted for so long, that they became selfish, and couldn't care less about the product. There was no teamwork, no family, no friends. That was the first time I had ever seen such a negative locker room dynamic in any company where I worked.

There was no morale. There was no team spirit. Everyone was miserable.

The saving grace for most involved was that, after the company had lost tens of millions of dollars, WCW was eventually sold for scrap to the WWF, and Vince McMahon picked up the contracts of more than half of its workers.

Chris and I had left the company prior to its demise, though, with me being part of a little scandal. Yeah, imagine that. I've always been the queen of controversy, right?

One TV taping, I can't remember where, I was pulled aside by the boss, Eric Bischoff.

Eric informed me that one of the girls in the locker room found a certain drug in one of the stalls in the women's bathroom and said I left it there.

The drug in question was the injectable painkiller Nubain.

I'll give you the 411 on Nubain. It is a synthetic morphine/heroin type drug only found in injectable form used to kill pain or, for addictive drug users, to get high. It is frequently found in California, sold out of back storage rooms of bodybuilding shops, and widely and frequently used by bodybuilders and fitness competitors.

Now, like I've said before, I've never been a recreational drug user. I was a heavy drinker and I took prescription pills. I have never smoked, snorted or shot *anything*!

But I was the accused; it didn't cross Bischoff's mind at all that he had a locker room full of fitness models who escorted Scott Steiner to the ring each night, and that it made much more sense that one of them would be using the drug.

Someone very persuasive must have told Bischoff it was mine.

I told him that it wasn't mine, that I didn't use Nubain, and I wanted to see the vial. He refused, and said he got rid of it.

I told him I'd pee in a cup right then and there to prove it wasn't mine. He then said he'd schedule me for a drug text in the morning and that I would be suspended until the results came back.

Great. Suspended. For something I didn't do. Guilty until proven innocent.

I wondered who could have disliked me enough to accuse me of this. Word of my suspension spread like wildfire in the locker room that night. Friends kept asking if I was OK and vented their frustration.

The next morning, I went and gave a urine sample. I knew I didn't have Nubain in my system but was a little worried about the quantity of pills I normally ingested. Later that day, I walked into the locker room and almost immediately was pulled aside by Torrie Wilson and Stacey Keibler. They asked me if I was OK.

"Yeah, but I'm suspended until my urine comes back negative," I said.

They said they had heard what happened and they knew who set me up: Kimberly Page.

Kimberly was married to "Diamond" Dallas Page at the time. She was initially brought into the company as the head of a dance troupe called "The Nitro Girls," who would perform dance routines in the ring at the beginning of every Nitro and between matches. She eventually started accompanying DDP to the ring as his valet after a short run with Johnny B. Badd. It was obvious that Kimberly didn't like me from day one. She was the top heel girl in the company, and when they brought me in as a heel, she felt threatened. She knew that I could get over as a heel more than anyone, and she was worried about me taking her spotlight.

She rarely spoke two words to me, but in hindsight, she really didn't speak to anyone in the locker room. Not even Miss Elizabeth, who was one of the sweetest ladies you could ever meet.

It was also very well known that Eric Bischoff and DDP were best friends and their wives were friends, as well. Too friendly, in fact, because it was also a well-known that Eric and Dallas would wife-swap.

Yep! They were swingers.

Kimberly was much better-looking than Eric's wife, so she had him wrapped around her little finger.

Kimberly went to Eric and told him it was my Nubain hoping to get me fired.

That rotten stinking bitch!

I wanted to kill her.

As soon as I found out it was Kim, I told some of the boys, including Scott Steiner.

Scott doesn't like many people, but if he likes you, he'll stand by you forever. He and I had been friends since I was 19 and he was coming by our Smoky Mountain shows in Marietta, Georgia.

Also, Scott is the last person you want to piss off. He had a very short fuse and an explosive temper. Needless to say, when I told him what Kimberly had done, he blew a fuse. His face got bright red and veins were popping out everywhere.

He stormed past me yelling, "Where is she? Where is that fucking whore, Kimberly?"

The boys that were in the hallway immediately glued themselves to the wall, anxious to get out of his line of fire.

He rushed straight into the girl locker room, despite many of the women being half-naked, he stood over Kimberly like Zeus hovering over the gods. He screamed at the top of his lungs at her, so loudly that most of his words were muffled, and you couldn't make out what he was saying.

The next thing we saw was Kimberly grabbing her suitcase and running down the hall and out the back door to the parking lot. He scared her so much he ran her out of the arena! But not only did she leave the arena, she left the company!

That was the night she quit and never returned, all because of Scott Steiner defending my honor. Dallas didn't even think about confronting him about the way he'd yelled at his wife. Neither did Eric. No one got in Scott's face, ever.

A week went by and I asked if my results were back. I was told no.

Another week passed and I was told by Eric that they misplaced my results. Great, more time off.

At the three-week mark, I was really pissed off. I stormed into Eric's office and demanded my results.

"Oh yeah. They were negative," he said in a very condescending voice, like he didn't have the time to deal with someone like me. "They came in a week ago, but I forgot about it."

That bastard! He just wanted me off TV and to not get paid for his own stubborn jollies and to pacify that two-faced bitch. He didn't want to admit he was wrong and he *definitely* didn't want to apologize—which he never has done, to this day.

Three weeks later, I was handed my release, anyway. Even though I had been falsely accused and tested negative, he couldn't face the fact that he had been wrong.

That is what makes Eric Bischoff Number Two on my Top Two list of people I can't stand.

Ironically, at WrestleMania 25, we were reluctantly forced to ride in the same limo together on our way to the arena from the hotel, along with a few other people. He was sitting right across from me, but did his best to avoid looking me in the eye.

Bastard. Karma's a bitch.

CHAPTER 22
WELCOME TO MY NIGHTMARE!

A couple months after I left WCW in 2000, Chris followed suit. We had never been more miserable working for any company in our entire lives than we had been there.

Chris had begun going back to Japan, this time for New Japan Pro Wrestling. Japanese tours are typically one month in length, every other month. They can be especially profitable for a wrestler, although it makes for a very lonely time for his spouse and family.

At the end of 2000, our house was finally sold, and we rented a small house on a little island right off of Atlantic City, New Jersey, called Brigantine. Brigantine was a cute little place, only two miles long and a half-mile wide, with a golf course in the center and the beach on the east coast. It was common to see more bicycles and boats than cars, even in the winter.

My best friend from high school, Stefanie, had a condo there, so I was well-acquainted with Brigantine from all of our trips there in our senior year.

It was beautiful, but there was one problem—we didn't know anyone and our families were more than an hour-and-a-half away. Chris got booked on a Japan tour that started the day after Christmas, 2000, and ended at the end of January, 2001. This would mark his first trip there since moving to Brigantine.

We always hated being apart, but this trip was especially hard for me.

I wasn't working. I wasn't even taking wrestling bookings. And I didn't know anyone. The only thing for me to do was eat, sleep... and drink, a lot.

I started drinking more and more to pass the time, to make those five long weeks go by faster. Eventually, alcohol took the place of my loneliness. I became extremely depressed in a very short time, so I drank to self-medicate.

I drank, and drank, and drank. I was going to the liquor store every day and bringing home a gallon jug of Dewar's scotch. I rode my bike there, even in the snow, because my driver's license was suspended. Nothing got in the way of me and my drink.

I was easily downing a full gallon of scotch a day, every day. And because I was filling up on liquor, not only did I not have an appetite, but I was way too drunk to eat. All I cared about was drinking and sleeping and hoping he would come home sooner with each passing day. One day, I got a bad stomachache, with diarrhea and vomiting. (Sorry; the details aren't pleasant). This was strange because I never got hung over or sick from scotch. I thought nothing of it, drank some Pepto Bismol and went to sleep.

The next day, I felt even worse. At this stage in my drinking, I wasn't even getting drunk anymore. I was just drinking to not feel sick. Maintaining.

Over the next four days, the pain in my abdomen worsened to where I couldn't eat, couldn't stand up, couldn't sleep, could barely breathe, but I still had the power to guzzle that scotch. The pain was so severe; it felt like someone had jammed a chainsaw into my gut and was tearing it up.

I had to crawl to the bathroom to poop. I kept a bucket near my bed to throw up into. I couldn't shower the whole time because I was so sick and in so much pain, so I smelled like shit and puke.

The pain felt like something punched a hole in me and set my guts on fire.

I would frequently pass out because the pain was so intense. I had never felt anything like it before in my life.

Finally, after six days of utter agony, I dialed 911. I couldn't take the pain anymore. After I called, I crawled out on my hands and knees to the front porch to get some cold air while I waited for the ambulance. I was sweating profusely from the pain and the high fever I was running. My breathing was horribly labored. I seriously thought I was dying.

And I was.

They rushed me to the hospital and took blood and ran tests right away. As they were moving me from the stretcher to the bed, I started to hyperventilate from the pain and eventually passed out cold.

Before I passed out, they asked me where my family and husband were. I was so out of it from the pain that I couldn't even remember my mom's phone number and all I could tell them about Chris was that he was somewhere in Japan.

When I woke up, I wasn't in the emergency room; I was in the Critical Care Unit. I had all kinds of wires and tubes attached to me and I had no idea where they came from.

162

How could all of this have happened? I just passed out.

Well, it was actually three days later. I was unconscious for three days, and Chris was at my bedside.

How the hell did he get there? All I knew to tell them at the hospital was he was in Japan. That's it. I knew the country he was in. And somehow they found him.

When my family came down to the hospital, they went to my house to try and locate a phone number to track him down in Japan. They couldn't find anything. Then, the phone rang. It was Chris calling for me! Thank God. My sister Lori told him bluntly, "Chris, you need to take the next plane home, because she only has about 48 hours to live, and she might not even make it through the night."

What? I had 48 hours to live? I might not even make it through the night? What in bloody hell was wrong with me?

All of their blood work and testing showed that I had a severe case of pancreatitis. Pancreatitis is the inflammation of your pancreas, caused by excessive alcohol consumption. And I had consumed a ton during those six days.

This is how your body metabolizes alcohol: After you drink it, it moves down the esophagus to the stomach, where it mixes with food and other fluids that you drink, diluting it. Then the diluted alcohol travels to your pancreas. Now, if there is no food or fluid in your stomach for it to dilute with (which there was none in mine for six days), it travels directly to your pancreas, becomes toxic, and your pancreas

163

blows up. This also leads to liver and kidney failure, which I also had.

Very quickly, my internal organs were dying; all of them.

I found out that the doctors sedated me when I arrived at the hospital, not only to deal with the pain, but in case my organs began to shut down, I wouldn't know, and I would die in comfort.

That's why it was three full days later before I came to.

I was going to die. They had a priest come in and read me my last rites, twice.

I was on my deathbed. Everyone came to the hospital—my family, Chris' family, friends. Everyone came to see me alive for the last time.

I had all kinds of tubes hooked up to me. My arms looked terrible. They had collapsed all the veins in my arms over a few days, so they had to go into my femoral vein with a catheter for my IV fluids. (The femoral vein is in your groin. They have to make an incision in your skin and the vein and thread a thick tube all the way up to your heart. Then they sew the little plastic contraption that attaches to the tube to your skin so it doesn't pull out. And yes, you are awake for all of this.)

I also had a Foley for the first time, a urinary catheter. That kind of freaked me out.

I wasn't allowed to get up to use the bathroom, so I had to poop right there in the makeshift diaper I was wearing. Even if I wanted to get up to use the bathroom, I wouldn't be physically able to.

There wasn't much poop though because I wasn't given any food. I was basically sustaining what little life I had left on the IV fluids.

I was in some seriously bad shape. For a week and a half, I was touch and go. I had so much morphine and Demerol running through my veins that I had no idea what was happening around me. I was even hallucinating from the drugs, and I was seeing little flying dragons all over my room.

Christopher stayed by my bedside 24-hours a day. He rarely slept. He didn't want to leave my side, just in case I died.

One night I told him to go home and get some sleep. I felt so bad for him; he had been at my side for more than a week and a half, living on hospital food. His eyes were dark and swollen and his body ached all over from sleeping in a chair for so long. I told him to go home, get some rest, and come back in the morning. Reluctantly, he did.

The next morning, around 8:00 a.m., I woke up. I just woke up and felt alert. I sat up in bed and pressed the call button for the nurse. The nurse came rushing in and asked me what was wrong. She was surprised to find me awake and coherent.

"Nothing is wrong," I said. "Where did Chris go? Can you hook up my phone so I can call him, please? Oh, and can you hook up the TV? I'm bored."

The nurse yelled, "Don't move!"

She left the room, and returned 30 seconds later with six other nurses and all 13 of my doctors. They were all looking at me, and then my charts, then back at me, and then back at my charts.

"This isn't the same person," one doctor said. "There is no way she could have recovered like this overnight."

But somehow, I did. I woke up that day with no

pain after I was in agony the night before. I was talking and moving fine, when the previous night I could only whisper and lay still. What could have happened overnight that brought me back from the brink of death?

I don't know. My doctors didn't know. No one knew. It was like an angel came down from heaven and healed me. It was a miracle.

No one could believe that the girl that was dying for a week-and-a-half was now on the phone, watching TV, and eating orange Jello.

I called Chris, and he answered in shock.

"Hey honey, where did you go last night? Are you coming back?"

"Don't move!" he said and hung up the phone.

About ten minutes later, he arrived at the hospital. He couldn't believe what he saw. No one could.

Over the next week, I was eating more and more solid food, and began putting some weight back on. I was emaciated from only being on fluids the whole time, but my face and head were swollen from the bloat. I was finally allowed to get out of bed, once I got some strength back, to finally move my bowels in a toilet, instead of my diaper.

I then decided that I didn't need the Foley catheter anymore, so I yanked it out.

Just a word of advice: *never* pull out your own catheter. It is held in place in your urethra by a hard balloon the size of a golf ball. It hurts *like hell* coming out! Let the nurse do it the right way, OK?

After two-and-a-half weeks in the hospital, my docs said that I could finally go home in a couple days, as long as everything was in order. My ridiculously

166

inflamed pancreas was back to normal and my liver and kidneys were finally functioning on their own again. They then told me that if I had waited only two or three more hours before calling 911, I would have died at home.

To this day, I am convinced that some supernatural entity saved my life. I feel that either my father or Stacey—or both of them—came to me and saved me. Something had to have. Because there is no logical or medical explanation as to why I bounced back from the dead.

I am eternally grateful to the doctors and nurses of the Atlantic City Medical Center, and to my darling Christopher, who never left my side.

Miracles do happen.

Every day of our lives.

CHAPTER 23
AYE DIOS MIO! USTEDES ESTAN LAS CUCARACHAS!

When I finally got out of the hospital, after three weeks of near-death misery, I had to take it easy. And not drink.

Not drinking was doctors' order number one. I was told that if I drank again, I would surely die. My pancreas wouldn't have the strength to recover a second time. There was too much damage done.

So Chris went back to work, but in this country. He didn't want to go back to Japan and risk something happening to me again while he was gone.

Me? I couldn't work at all since I was so weakened by my condition. I even had to go to a beauty salon and get all my hair cut off, because the back of my head was so matted from lying in bed for three weeks. No comb or conditioner would get through the tangled mess.

When you go from working in a million dollar company to working independent shows in this business, it's a shock to your financial stability. We had already lost so much money on our house, and now we were trying to make ends meet with only one income.

The independent scene is like the stock market. Sometimes things can be profitable for a few months, and then it can crash... hard. It is very unpredictable.

There were months that the amount of money Chris was bringing home wasn't even enough to cover all of our bills. We had to dip into our dwindling savings account some more.

The winter of 2002 came fast, and we were almost broke. Our lease was almost up, and we weren't sure where we were going to go.

That's when Chris got a phone call from Victor Quinones, in Puerto Rico. Victor was the owner of the International Wrestling Association there, and we had known him from our trip to Japan for Michinoku Pro Wrestling back in 1997. Victor was a really nice guy who always liked both of us, and he was very "out of the closet." He would make jokes with some of the boys about his homosexuality, and no one ever took offense to it. He liked to throw his money around and impress people with his generosity. Everyone genuinely liked him.

Chris was offered a job with the IWA starting in April.

Fabulous!

This couldn't have had better timing. This meant we had to move to Puerto Rico, but where would we go on the meantime?

We decided to put our things in storage and stay with Chris' family until we left for Puerto Rico. In the meantime, word got around that Chris was going to start for the IWA, and one day he got another phone call. This time is was his good friend, Sabu.

Sabu is the nephew of the original hardcore

legend, the Sheik. The Sheik made a name for himself in the 60's, 70's and 80's as one of the most violent, bloodthirsty wrestlers in the world. He carved a niche for himself in Japan and Puerto Rico, where extremely violent matches were predominant.

In Puerto Rico, he worked primarily for Carlos Colon and the World Wrestling Council, the main competitor to the IWA. His was also the promotion in which the legendary Bruiser Brody was killed in a locker room shower.

Carlos had heard about Chris going to Puerto Rico, so he called in a favor to the Sheik, who asked Sabu to call Chris. They wanted to know if Chris would go to work for Carlos instead of the IWA, because they were lacking the talent needed to surpass the IWA in ticket sales.

Chris, being the loyal friend that he was, told Sabu and the Sheik that he would go to Puerto Rico for Carlos instead, and that I would come along with him as a package deal.

We packed up and headed to Puerto Rico in April of 2003. I was SO looking forward to this. I had always been a beach lover, so the chance to live on a beautiful, tropical island was a dream come true.

And the plan was to live there for two years. Perfect!

When we got to Puerto Rico, we went to the hotel that the Americans working for both companies stayed. It was called the Empress Hotel in Isla Verde, and it wasn't quite the tropical paradise that we expected.

It was a rundown slum of a motel on the beach, with beds that felt like they were 50 years old, and

170

only half the rooms had TVs. The one redeeming quality it had was a restaurant that kicked ass! They had a good-sized menu, and everything on it was incredible. There was an old Italian man who ran the restaurant and managed the hotel named Mr. Carl Palermo, who instantly took a liking to us; especially since Chris had an Italian last name.

We were promised $800 per week, and we started to look for an apartment while we stayed at the Empress. We were excited to get started working and enjoy our new island lifestyle. The problem was, our tropical dreams were just that—dreams. Dreams that would soon turn into a nightmare.

For the first four weeks, we worked every show and got paid our guarantee. The shows were a little different than what we were used to. They were mostly outdoor shows, in open-air baseball parks. The locker rooms were hot, sticky, and filthy. The fans were barbaric. They believed in heels and babyfaces, and it was common to have 9-volt batteries and cups of urine propelled at your head.

Yes, I said cups of urine. Puerto Rican pee pee.

At these baseball parks, the dugouts were locker rooms and the fans were right above them. As you left the dugout you had to sprint past the fans, or you would get doused with piss.

Barbaric.

After our first month there, we found our apartment. It was beautiful. One bedroom, on the fourth floor in a five-floor apartment building on the beach in Isla Verde. It was furnished with beautiful furniture that had a Spanish flair, which I loved. A mango tree hung over the balcony, providing fresh fruit and fragrance daily. The bedroom had a view of the blue green waters of the Caribbean Sea. The slatted windows allowed cool ocean breezes into the bedroom and living room.

The problem was you had to stay on the beach or in the apartment for the beauty of Puerto Rico, because the rest of it was not so nice.

OK, it was pretty friggin' disgusting.

My apologies to anyone reading who hails from there, or lives there currently.

If you go there on vacation, you stay in a gorgeous resort, and you never get to see the "real" Puerto Rico. If you live there, you do.

When we left the apartment we had to walk five blocks up to the main road to the bus stop. We took a bus into the city of Santurce in San Juan every Monday to go to the office to film promos and get paid. On the walk to the bus stop, the streets were filthy. There was raw sewage flowing down two blocks of street along the curb. The stench was vile and overwhelming.

When we got on the bus, it was always overcrowded, with standing room only. We had to drive through a huge metal fence, into the projects, and out the other side on our way to Santurce. One particular ride through the projects was eventful. We drove up upon a large group of people standing in a circle facing outwards. In the middle, was the local drug lord, shot 12 times in the face. His guts and brains were splattered all over the pavement. The people circled him so the police couldn't get through to him. Street justice. They eventually had to call in a S.W.A.T. team and riot squad to recover the body.

172

When we got to the bus stop in Santurce, we had to walk seven blocks along a tree-lined street in the middle of the business section of town. That seemed innocent enough, but there were dirty syringes stuck in every tree.

Basically, the "real" Puerto Rico is disgusting.

There is so much filth, crime, poverty, and drug use that it makes the island almost uncivilized. It was very common to walk down the street and pass someone sitting on the curb shooting up heroin.

Like the saying goes: it's a nice place to visit, but you wouldn't want to live there!

After we settled into our apartment, things started to change. Paychecks were late. Very late. And short. Our $800 per week became $600, then $400, then $200. We got paid weekly if we were lucky. Sometimes they wouldn't have the money one week, and would promise to make it up the following week, which never happened.

Carlos had a "partner" named Victor Jovica. What we found out later was that Jovica was the real owner and Carlos was just the figurehead, on a small salary just like the rest of us. Then we started getting weekly pay in the amount of $50, we thought it couldn't get any worse.

A bunch of us wanted to "strike" and not wrestle until we got paid, but when it came down to it, they didn't have the balls to stick to their guns.

Jovica was as slimy as slimy comes. At the shows, he would give the boys empanadillas and beer in place of money. Some of the Puerto Rican guys were happy with that, usually the ones who weren't getting paid.

173

We were draining our savings account more and more, until eventually we couldn't make the $1,000 per month rent and got evicted.

Then, we were back at the Empress. Mr. Palermo gave us a room at no charge. And he would cook special meals for us in the kitchen.

He was very generous, and he knew the type of scum we were dealing with in Colon and Jovica. We wondered how he could afford to give us a free room for two months and all the food we could eat for free. Well, we later discovered that Mr. Palermo was running the hotel and restaurant for the Mafia, so it was used as a way to launder money and would never go out of business.

Thank God Chris had that Italian last name! (Even though there wasn't an ounce of Italian in him; he was Slovak!)

After six months, I told Chris I just couldn't do it anymore. We were living on minimal food, and lost some of our belongings when we were evicted. I was leaving Puerto Rico, with or without him. I couldn't handle how horrific this place was. I wanted out.

We gave Carlos our notice and a list of the paychecks we were short or missing. He said he'd buy our plane tickets and give us the money we were owed.

A week and a half went by, and nothing.

Finally we went to the office, hellbent and pissed off. He told us he couldn't afford the tickets, but if we worked another show, he'd pay us.

OK, we would work another show, but this time I had a little something up my sleeve, in the form of a payback.

174

It was a TV taping, so the ring truck and the production truck were both there… and so were the keys to the truck, left in the ignition. And we were a good four-hour drive from the studio.

When all attention was on the show and not the trucks, I took the keys out of the ignition and threw them in my purse. At the end of the show, they had no way to get the trucks started. I had the only set of keys!

When, I got back to Isla Verde, I took a moonlit stroll on the beach, made a wish, and threw the keys straight into the ocean.

Ha! They don't fuck with me and get away with it!

That week, we were given $200 (instead of the $3,000 we were owed) and our plane tickets.

Carlos got away scot free on the plane tickets, though. He had to use his daughter's credit card to buy them.

Pathetic. Just pathetic.

We left Puerto Rico and never looked back.

Years later, in 2011, I ran into Carlos Colon for the first time since we'd left. It was at the WrestleMania after-party, and I was behind him on line for a drink at the bar.

As he turned around and was face-to-face with me, his black face turned ghostly white from embarrassment. He was speechless. He didn't know if he could, or should say anything to me.

But this was the weekend I was inducted into the WWE Hall of Fame, so I was the bigger person and remained civil, knowing that I got him with the keys back in 2003.

Karma.

175

CHAPTER 24
ONLY THE GOOD DIE YOUNG

Leaving Puerto Rico was the best thing we could have done. It was truly Hell on Earth. That's where I started drinking again and, with somas being sold over the counter for a quarter each, it would have been too easy to fall back into the depths of addiction.

The problem with coming home was that we were now broke. We had very little money left after trying to survive for six months on that island. We had to use our own money there, because if we didn't, we had only enough money from our pay to eat, once a day.

So, we came home and went to live with my mother again. It was hard to do, but we really didn't have a choice.

Chris started working indies again, but our experience in Puerto Rico soured me on the business to the point that I wanted nothing to do with it. I took some time off.

I took a job at a friend's tanning salon as his manager. The shop was just around the corner from my mother's house, and I was getting decent money to run the place.

Another reason I didn't work in the business at

this time was because my weight had been drastically affected by the pancreatitis.

See, your pancreas directly affects your insulin production, and your insulin levels have a direct impact on your weight. So over the three years since I was sick, my weight skyrocketed—hitting 187 pounds at one point.

This was incredibly hard for me, especially since every wrestling website was so happy to report how much weight I had gained, speculating my over-eating and saying I "let myself go." Never once did they stop and think I might have had a medical issue that caused the weight gain, which I had no control over.

The website's so-called "journalists" and fans around the world were so incredibly cruel, insensitive, and ruthless in their negative and demeaning comments about me. I was eventually forced to get rid of my computer and hole up at home.

It was awful.

A once confident, outgoing, beautiful woman, who was lusted after for years by men all over the world, and now a depressed recluse, too afraid to go anywhere, fearful that she might be recognized. Going to the grocery store was a scary thing. Walking the mall was terrifying. Going to the gym was brutal, because people expected to see the body I had in the '90s and my pre-pancreatitis curves.

I grew deeply depressed and self-conscious. My self-esteem was gone.

Do you have any idea what it's like for someone to recognize you, and then ask, "What happened to you?" Those same people don't even bother to try to hide the confusion and disgust in their face? It feels awful.

I would cry when I tried on clothes, and mostly lived in sweatpants. I just wanted to hide in my bedroom, and I rarely went to indies with Chris.

Then Chris got a phone call from a new company called TNA, Total Nonstop Action. They had been around for a year or so, and were on TV nationwide. The Jarretts and the Carters, Bob and Dixie owned them. Bob Carter is the owner of Panda Energy, who supplies energy and electricity to a large part of the country. He needed something to be a tax write-off, so he bought into TNA and gave it to his daughter, Dixie, to run.

The booker at the time was "The American Dream" Dusty Rhodes and he had always liked Chris. Most of the older guys liked him, because he was very "old school" himself and had the utmost respect for his seniors.

When Chris got the call from Dusty, he couldn't have been more excited. TNA had focused on smaller, technically sound wrestlers and their light-heavyweight (X Division) division was the feature of their program. It was the first time a wrestling promotion featured the smaller guys over heavyweight monsters, and it was working. The highest ratings the show got was for the X Division wrestlers and the girls, the TNA Knockouts.

Chris was psyched. As a smaller guy, he had always been put on the back burner. This was his opportunity to shine.

When he started, he was on Cloud 9. He hung out with Dusty a lot, and was asked for ideas for finishes almost nightly.

He started dressing differently. The days of wearing gym attire to shows were gone. He now wore dress pants and nice buttoned down shirts to work.

178

Dusty even likened him to his idol, Ric Flair, at one TV taping, saying, "Lookie here! Candido thinks he's the Nature Boy with them snazzy clothes."

That made Chris' day.

He was in his element. This was where he needed to work. He was finally happy, after so many years, and earning the respect he deserved.

The pay wasn't fantastic, but it was enough to pay our bills and get out of the hole a little bit. A few months went by where he would fly to Orlando each week for TV tapings. Every time he came home, he had a bigger smile on his face than the week before, and more great stories to tell me.

A PPV was coming up, and he was scheduled to be in a tag team match with Lance Hoyt taking on Gran Apollo and Sonny Siaki. I packed his bags, drove him to the airport, and sent him off to work. He kissed me goodbye as usual. We told each other we loved each other, and I said to him what I always said before a match: "Be careful."

It was the night of the Lockdown PPV, April 24th, 2005, but I didn't order it. I never really watched wrestling while I was working, and I especially wasn't going to watch it now with the sour taste left in my mouth from Puerto Rico.

I did what he and I would always do on a boring weekend night. I decided to take a drive into Manhattan and get a pizza and some pastries. Before the match, Chris called me, as usual. Everything was normal. He told me it was going to be an easy match.

About 30 minutes later, as I was walking out of Ray's Pizza on Ninth Avenue, my phone rang.

It was Chris. And he sounded frantic.

179

He tells me he broke his ankle in the match and he's on his way to the hospital.

I asked him how bad it was.

"Pretty bad," he said.

Well, pretty bad was the understatement of the year. It was so badly broken that his whole foot was pointed outward and he couldn't feel his toes. It was a freak injury. He took a bump off a dropkick from Siaki and his right leg crashed into Siaki and folded back underneath him as he landed. When they X-rayed it at the hospital, they found he broke both his tibia and fibula, and dislocated his ankle. They told him he needed surgery, and they would have to put in two titanium plates and numerous screws.

Great.

He had been lucky so far in his career. He'd had a lot of injuries, but hadn't needed any surgery thus far.

He went into the operating room, and I nervously awaited a call from anyone telling me he was out of surgery and in recovery.

I eventually got word that the surgery was a success, and that he was coming home a couple days later.

The next day he managed the tag team Naturals (Andy Douglas and Chase Stevens) to the TNA tag team championships on TV, with his leg in a cast and on crutches.

When I picked him up at the airport, he was waiting for me by baggage claim in a wheelchair. He was upset. He felt as if his dreams were just shattered, that he would never make it back to TNA.

I took him home, he took the prescriptions the doctors gave him, and he went to sleep.

The next day, he woke up in a lot of pain. We

couldn't understand why the pain was worse except for the fact that the anesthesia had finally all worn off. So he did what any wrestler would do after an injury.

More pain. More pain pills.

On the second day home, the pain was unbearable. I asked him if he wanted to go to the hospital, and he said no. Chris never liked going to see a doctor, so there was no way I could persuade him to go.

As the day went on, he took more pills to counter the horrific pain. It was too much for him to handle, and he cried most of the time. Around 4:00 p.m., he went to sleep. About an hour later, I tried to wake him up, but it seemed like he was out cold. His breathing had a funny sound to it—it was labored and congested.

I didn't like what I saw or heard.

I finally got him to wake up and come around, but he faded out again almost instantly.

Something wasn't right. He couldn't breathe.

On top of all that, his foot and upper leg were extremely swollen around the cast he was wearing.

That was when I called 911. I had been pre-med in college, so I knew enough to know that there was definitely something wrong with his breathing.

I rode in the ambulance to the hospital, and my mom followed us. His father met us there, and when we arrived, they brought Chris straight into a trauma room.

He was still in and out of consciousness. I was telling him I loved him and I was trying to get him to say he loved me, too. After a few minutes of begging him, he finally got up enough strength to whisper, "I love you."

Those would be his last words.

The three of us went into a small waiting room around the corner so they could get to work on him.

We sat there scared to death, wondering what was going on, wondering what was wrong with him.

Ten minutes went by and the doctor walked in the room.

"Mrs. Candido?" he said.

"Yes."

"I'm sorry. He's gone."

What? What do you mean, "gone?" He had to be OK, I thought. I pushed past the doctor and rounded the corner and rushed to Chris' side.

He was gone.

I turned to the doctor and started pounding on his chest, demanding that he do something—something to bring him back.

He held me and said, "I'm sorry, we did everything we could."

No! He can't be gone! He is my husband, my best friend. We were just over a month away from our 16-year anniversary.

What was I going to do without him?

I was in total shock. I didn't believe he was dead. I *refused* to believe it. I searched for his pulse—nothing. I listened for his breath—nothing. I lifted his eyelid—his pupils were dark, fixed and dilated.

He was gone.

That was April 28, 2005.

Christopher Barrett Candido was only 33 years old.

I couldn't believe my ears when the doctor told me what had happened.

First, he had pneumonia. Pneumonia is a very common occurrence post-surgery because of the general anesthetic administered. That explained his difficulty in breathing.

What they told me next, I couldn't believe.

The cause of death was a blood clot.

A blood clot formed in his ankle, dislodged, and traveled to his heart, causing a heart attack. But what could have caused a blood clot in an otherwise healthy 33 year-old male?

It turns out blood clots are possible after surgery and can be treated, if the blood clot isn't in an accelerated dislodged state. High altitudes can cause the clot and accelerate it through the circulatory system.

Christopher flew home at 36,000 feet two days following the surgery.

The thing that bothered me was I didn't know if anyone at the hospital in Florida told him not to fly. I don't even know if they knew he had to fly home to New Jersey.

If we had known, there were a ton of friends he could have stayed with for a week or two in Florida, if necessary. If we had known this, we may have been able to prevent his death, but no one knew.

It was hands-down the single worst night of my life. Christopher was the most important thing in my life. We had spent half of our lives together.

He was my best friend.

I was a basket case. I couldn't imagine life without him. I had spent my entire adult life—17 years old to 32 years old—with him, and I was lost without him.

Over the next week, things got worse.

When it was time to make his final arrangements, I was supposed to meet his father, step-mother, mother, and step-father at the funeral home to decide what was going to be done.

When I got there, the decision was already made

183

by the four of them to have him cremated.

Cremated? That was something Chris didn't believe in. He believed in a burial.

But his parents were looking out for their own selfish needs and wanted to split the ashes between them. They didn't even ask my opinion. They acted like it didn't matter what I thought.

When the wake and funeral came, I couldn't believe the turn-out. Over a thousand people came—friends, family, fans, and the entire TNA crew, including Bob and Dixie Carter. Most of the old ECW crew was there, some WWE and WCW guys, and legends like Terry Funk also showed up.

It was really overwhelming. There was a line of people wrapped around the funeral home waiting to get in.

At one point I walked up to Chris, leaned over him, and whispered to him.

"Look baby. Look how many people love you. You sold the place out."

I don't think Chris ever knew how many people loved and respected him and cared about him. If he could see all these people, he would have been in shock!

But then again, he saw them. Each and every one.

At the last viewing at the funeral home, someone said something to me that drove a dagger deep into my heart.

Chris' mother.

She walked up to me and said, "This is all your fault. You could have prevented this if you got him to the hospital sooner. This should have been you, not my son."

This woman, who had been like a mother to me, was my family for 16 years, and now she has all this hatred towards me and wished I was dead?

My heart sunk. I couldn't believe she could be so cruel. I understand she was grieving the loss of her son, but I was grieving, too … maybe more.

After the funeral, Chris' final paycheck from TNA came in the mail. He was paid $1,500 for that last PPV match. I went to the bank to deposit it, but even with his ID, they wouldn't let me endorse the check.

I called the TNA office to tell them my situation. I told them I needed them to cut me his final paycheck in my name so I could pay off some of his bills. We had a shared bank account and shared credit cards, so I was responsible for his bills.

Terry Taylor called me back two days later and said they couldn't cut me a check in my name because he and I were never legally married. I was shit out of luck, and stuck with the bills.

If you think about it, Chris lost his life for free. His final match where he broke his ankle—which was the root cause of his death—was literally for nothing.

I hated the company after that point. A company that I had raved about and put over left and right as the greatest thing on TV had screwed me and, essentially, Chris as well.

I couldn't believe the gall of these people.

But they did send me something during the days of the funeral…

A ham.

They sent me a ham.

A "condolences ham."

From the home delivery store, Heavenly Hams.

Yep, they couldn't send me his last paycheck, but hey, I got a ham! I should be more than pleased and grateful for their thoughtfulness.

Maybe if I sliced the ham and sent pieces out in envelopes to credit card companies, they would have accepted that as payment.

I could have included a post-it note saying, "I'm so sorry I can't send you a check, but please accept this slice of ham as payment for March."

That would have worked, right?

After all, the TNA office sure as hell thought that sending me a ham would make up for my grief and loss!

"Oh, I just lost my husband and best friend, but *fuck*, I got me a ham!"

Needless to say, I threw the ham out.

I couldn't fathom how insensitive they could be.

Even after, at the funeral, Dixie Carter pulled me aside and said, "If there is anything you need, anything I could do for you, you just call me."

Well, where the fuck is his last $1,500, bitch??

I guess you can say I'm a little bitter. Just a little bit.

You can also rest assured that I will never, ever, take a job with TNA. I lost all respect for that company, and I doubt if I'll ever respect it again.

I miss you and love you, Christopher.

You are always on my mind.

RIP Christopher Barrett Candido, 3-21-72 to 4-28-05

CHAPTER 25
STARTING OVER

Losing Chris gutted me, absolutely gutted me. Never in my life had I been alone. I didn't know how to function. I didn't know how to live. I had spent the first 17 years of my life with my parents, and the last 16 years with Chris. I was lost. I felt like an orphan.

I had now lost the three most important people in my life—my father, my niece, and now Chris.

I felt like I had nothing and no one left. The trauma I was going through was tremendous. I didn't know how to deal with it all, so I turned to self-medicating, again. I picked up the bottle.

I was in a deep depression for a few months. All I did was lay in bed, watch TV, and drink. I couldn't even cook for myself. I couldn't get to the gym. It was a struggle to even leave the house to go grocery shopping.

I was a mess.

Four months went by and I had to do something to get out of this funk I was in. I started going back to the gym a couple days a week, and one day I asked if they needed any help. They did. They needed someone in membership sales. I had worked in a gym while I was in college, so I figured it would be good to get me out of the house and get my mind on something else for a change.

I started that September, and by November, I was the number one salesperson in the district, which included 24 gyms.

When I do something, I really do it. I put 200% into it. Instead of working my 40 hour work week, I was doing 60-70 hours. Being at the gym so much kept my mind off of losing Chris, and allowed me to heal a little bit.

In January, 2006, I met my new boyfriend, John, through mutual friends at the gym. I wasn't looking for a relationship so soon, but sometimes things just happen. When we met, he wasn't exactly my type, but after our first date, I was crazy about him.

Two weeks later, I got his last name tattooed on my tailbone (which has since been covered up) and a month after that we got an apartment together. We moved really fast, and we were in love.

I told you I do everything 200%!

John is the one who gets the credit for getting me back in the gym, back on my diet, and back in "Sunny shape."

This was evident less than two years later, when on December 10, 2007, I was asked by the WWE to make an appearance on the Monday Night RAW 15th anniversary show.

I was excited, but I was also extremely nervous, because it would be the first time I was to step into that locker room since 1998... and it would also be the first time I saw Shawn since I left the company.

In fact, that is what I was more nervous about—seeing Shawn. Walking down to the ring in front of 25,000 people was old hat. I could do that in my sleep. It felt incredibly awkward to see Shawn again.

They called me three and a half weeks before the

show. I got on the scale and I was 150 pounds. I looked good for a girl working at a gym, but not good enough for an appearance on TV.

So John formulated a strict diet for me, upped my cardio, and in three and a half weeks I lost 17 pounds!

A woman who weighed 187 pounds just a year and a half prior now weighed just 133!

I couldn't believe I had done it. It took six years for my pancreas and insulin to finally regulate so I could drop all the weight I gained from my pancreatitis, but I did it!

I was so proud of myself. It was the new me. I figured I'd try and start taking bookings again.

I couldn't believe how fast they were coming in! I was getting booked every weekend again.

I was working for everyone from Ring of Honor to the NWS back in New Jersey, and everyone in between.

I was back!

And I was finally happy again.

It took a very long time to heal and get out of my depression, but with John's help, and time, I was able to break free.

The WWE show date arrived, and we got in the car and headed up to Bridgeport, Connecticut. I was fine for the entire two-hour ride until we were about ten minutes from the building. That's when my anxiety rose, my stomach was nauseous, and my hands became sweaty. I couldn't believe I was this nervous all because of a man!

But this wasn't just any man; this was the only man to have broken my heart.

My heart was throbbing in my chest when we walked inside the arena, but as soon as I saw the first person—my old make-up girl, Jill Getlan—all my nerves subsided and I felt like I was home again.

189

Jill greeted me with a huge hug and kiss, and then other members of the production staff began to flock to me to say hello. It was such a great feeling to be welcomed back by everyone. I saw a lot of the boys I already knew, and most of the younger guys came up to me and introduced themselves.

John and I proceeded to catering where we got on line for lunch. When we chose our table, Ric Flair and CM Punk sat down with us.

I've known Ric for years now, but I hadn't seen Punk for about nine years, and that was only once on an indie show. As it turns out, Chris was CM Punk's idol, and when he passed away, Punk got a tattoo for Chris that read "No Gimmicks Needed," which was Chris' moniker through ECW and WCW.

I went back to the catering line for some more protein and while I was grabbing a piece of grilled chicken, I felt a tap on my shoulder. I turned around and, OH MY GOD!

I was face to face with Shawn for the first time in nine years.

OMG! What was I to do? I didn't have to think of what to do because he grabbed me and gave me the biggest hug of the day.

Wow! Talk about awkward! There I am in the arms of the one man I loved and couldn't have, while my current boyfriend was sitting at a table with Ric Flair watching every bit of it.

Shawn released me from his bear hug and looked me over.

"Wow! You look amazing," he said. "You look exactly the same!"

"Thanks! So do you! You haven't changed a bit," I said.

OK, so I lied through my teeth.

He didn't quite look the same. He looked aged and weathered, but still handsome. But hey, a little white lie never hurt anyone.

Later that night, as the show began, I waited at the curtain for my big entrance.

I was involved in the first segment of the night with Vince, his daughter (Stephanie), son (Shane), and Triple-H. Triple-H was on the microphone and when my music hit, the energy that flowed through my body was electrifying. Triple-H introduced me as "The Original Diva, Sunny," and I made my way to the ring.

It was amazing! I was back! It felt like I never left.

This opened the door for more return appearances. I was so very well received at RAW that they knew they could use me on more shows.

It was late winter, 2009, when I got a phone call from John Laurinaitis.

John is the younger brother of Animal, known from his days in the ring as Johnny Ace, and was then the head of talent relations for the WWE. He called about the upcoming WrestleMania PPV from Houston, Texas in April of 2009.

They were having a 25 Diva battle royal, and he thought it would only be right to have me involved. I jumped at the chance, told him I'd love to do it, and then hung up the phone.

Then I thought to myself, "Wait a minute. I'm not a wrestler, I've never been in a battle royal, and I've never gone over the tope rope."

Well, I'd have to learn quickly because I had just agreed to do it.

The day came and I was filled with anticipation.

Kid Rock was the special musical guest and he was to sing on the ramp while all the girls made their entrances. As I walked past Kid Rock, I turned around in front of him, and opened my robe as if I flashed him. Then I threw it off to the side and got into the ring.

This match was destined to be a clusterfuck from the very beginning. We had 25 girls in there, and there may have been five of us that actually knew how to wrestle; and I'm not a wrestler. The rest were clumsy, careless bikini models, and there was no way I was going to get injured by any of them.

I was supposed to be the ninth eliminated, but I figured if I sped that up a little bit, I could get out sooner, avoid injury, and be in the locker room changing before the nine-minute match was over.

And I did.

I started off with someone I knew would be "safe"—Victoria. She and I got along very well, and I trusted her to do right by me. Next up, I had to beat on Maryse a little. She was to have no offense and just sell for me. Out of nowhere, I saw her foot coming right at my face. Thank God I have quick reflexes, as I just narrowly avoided a broken nose. Lastly, I was to go back and forth with Beth Phoenix, whom I also trusted, until she tossed me out of the ring.

I ended up eliminating myself fourth instead of ninth, with my good friend Torrie Wilson right behind me.

She and I helped each other up and limped down the aisle together in defeat.

Whew! Thank God that was over and I came out unscathed!

With these two appearances, I showed the world

that Sunny was back in the saddle. The "Original Diva" had returned, better than ever.

What was to come next *completely* took me by surprise.

I was about to make history, yet again.

CHAPTER 26
THE CREAM ALWAYS RISES

There has always been speculation of when—not "if"—I would get inducted into the WWE Hall of Fame.

To those of us in this crazy business, it is the pinnacle of our careers; the top of the top.

Once you've gotten to the Hall of Fame, there is not much better you can do.

In 1996 at 23 years old, I was the youngest performer ever to be inducted into the Cauliflower Alley Club Hall of Fame. The CAC is more or less our industry Hall of Fame, well known by us insiders, but not very publicly known (kind of like the SAG awards as opposed to the Oscars).

In 1996, Vince asked me if I'd like to go to the CAC banquet and represent the company along with him, his wife Linda, Jim Cornette, Chris and a few others. Of course I said yes, but I thought I was just attending. I had no idea I was going there for other reasons.

All night long at the banquet, people were getting inducted and receiving awards for their achievements in pro-wrestling. I wasn't paying very much attention as I was noshing on my dinner.

I was halfway through my piece of cake when Freddie Blassie was on the stage talking about the next inductee, the Manager of the Year, when all of a sudden, Chris and Jim Cornette start saying, "Go! Tammy, go up there!"

"For what?"

"They just announced your name! You're being inducted!"

Oh my God! Are you kidding me? I'm getting inducted into the CAC Hall of Fame?

Holy Crap! I'm only 23! I thought only the old timers got inducted! OMG!

Well, the CAC committee agreed I was ready for it.

So I went on stage, took the microphone, and gave them the most improv on-the-fly acceptance speech they had ever heard. I glanced over to our dinner table and there were Vince and Linda beaming with pride, and chuckling inside because they had just gotten me with this surprise.

It wasn't easy to give an eloquent speech on the spur of the moment, but I did my best, and I guess my best was good enough, because I got a standing ovation.

Wow! I was in a Hall of Fame at 23 years old! This was a first in CAC history! I was extremely proud of that honor, and I still display my CAC award on my wall to this day.

Fast forward 15 years later, just after New Year's, 2011.

John and I were preparing to leave for our yearly trip to Riviera Maya, Mexico. It was a Monday night. John was at MMA class and I was home cleaning and packing for our flight to Mexico the following morning.

It was about 9:15 p.m. on January 10, and the phone rang. My caller ID said "Johnny Ace."

What was Ace doing calling me at 9:15 on a Monday night? Shouldn't he be at RAW?

I picked up and said hello, and asked what was up. Ace made some small talk with me about the weather, what I was doing, and about my upcoming trip to Mexico. It was strange to me, because Ace never called just for the hell of it, especially when RAW was on live.

He then asked if I was watching RAW. I said I had it on TV, but I wasn't really paying attention because I was elbow-deep in suitcases.

"Well, sit down, and watch now," he said.

I took a break, sat down, and turned my focus to the television. A segment began announcing the induction that April of Shawn Michaels into the WWE Hall of Fame.

After the five-minute segment, I turned my attention back to the phone, and Ace.

"Good for him!" I said. "If anyone deserves to be in the Hall of Fame, it's Shawn. I'm so happy for him."

Then I thought, "What does this have to do with me?"

"Well," Ace said, "let me tell you why I'm calling."

Finally. Get to the point. Ace always has an agenda.

"We'd like you to be the second inductee into the Hall of Fame this year."

My jaw dropped. I was stunned into silence. I couldn't believe what I had just heard. He had to be just messing with me.

After what felt like a year's worth of silence, I said the only thing I could think to say.

"You're shitting me, right?"

196

"No, I'm not shitting you," he replied with a chuckle. "We were discussing who we should induct this year and Vince thought it should be your year."

Oh my God! Shut the front door!

My silence and disbelief quickly turned to tears and happiness. Then I tried to give him every reason why he should *not* induct me.

"Don't you think I'm too young? Are you sure? Have you really thought this over? There has to be someone more deserving."

He stopped me.

"Nope, we are sure it's your year and you deserve it," he said. "Now, we want to keep it a secret so don't tell anyone until we announce it on TV. Well, you can tell your boyfriend, but that's it."

"OK, Ace, no problem. My lips are sealed. Thank you so much!"

With that, I hung up the phone.

I started tearing up, screaming, laughing. Every emotion came rushing over my body, one blurring into the next.

OMG! It's really happening! I have to tell somebody! Anybody!

But I couldn't. John was at MMA class and never brought his phone in. I was literally shaking with excitement. I had such a strong need to tell someone, to let them share in my joy and accomplishment.

But who?

I picked up the phone and called my longtime friend and photographer, Bob Mulrenin. Bob is a great guy, who I affectionately call "Uncle Bob." This is the man who had consistently taken the most amazing pictures of me over the last seven years.

He was so psyched for me when I told him. And I felt so much better that I let the cat out of the bag. But I needed to limit it to Bob and John and keep it quiet until the company announced it publicly.

When John came home and I told him the news, he was ecstatic. He couldn't be happier for me. It was such a great was to start off our vacation.

When we came back from Mexico, I made sure I watched RAW every Monday, waiting to see them announce me as the next inductee.

Ace had told me they would give me a heads up so I would know when to tune in.

Monday after Monday went by. No heads up. No announcement.

Meanwhile, I decided that I had to get in the best shape of my life for the Hall of Fame ceremony, because for the pinnacle of my career, I should naturally look the best I ever had.

It is all too common for inductees to show up at their induction looking like a shell of their former selves. After all, you are usually 50 years old—or dead—but the time you get inducted.

I wanted to show up gorgeous and reinvented, in better shape than I had been in in my prime in my mid to late-20's.

I was 38 years old. The youngest and only the fifth woman to ever be inducted into the Hall of Fame, and I had something to prove.

This was my chance to tell the world to kiss my royal behind.

Well, not ALL the world; just all the negative assholes that had ridiculed me over the years for my weight gain and periods of unemployment. This was my shot to shove it up all their asses and walk away with my head held high, and to walk away the better person.

All of those fans, wrestlers and website writers that loved to badmouth me and kick me when I was down, could eat their words when I walk out on that stage, looking phenomenal!

I really needed John to push me hard now. I had just 11-weeks to get in the best shape of my life, so out with the carbs and up with the cardio!

Right then and there, I stopped eating carbs, *all* carbs! I wouldn't see a potato, pasta, rice, or bread for 11 weeks. At the gym, I upped my cardio on the treadmill from 30-minutes to two hours running interval sprints, and shortened my weight lifting to 30-minutes with lighter weights. I also started training Muay Thai kickboxing.

Let me tell you, 20 minutes of Thai burns more calories than two hours on the treadmill! It's grueling, but so worth it.

Two months had passed by, and still no heads up. I was starting to wonder if they really were shitting me. I decided not to go dress shopping until the announcement was made, and not until I was close to my final weight and dress size.

It was Monday, March 7, when I finally got "the call." My announcement was going to be on RAW that night. John and I asked a couple of friends if they wanted to join us at Buffalo Wild Wings to watch it all go down. I was sitting at the table eating mini corndogs when the segment came on.

It was absolutely amazing! And tear jerking! I started to cry like a baby! I was so happy.

I couldn't believe that I got to that point in my career at 38 years old. I couldn't believe the WWE was actually going to bestow that honor upon me.

Now I was just over three weeks away from the big day. Waiting for the announcement to finally air was murder, but the real murder was going to be my final three weeks training in preparation for my moment.

I started wearing a vinyl sauna suit while doing cardio. I added in more spin classes, up to three-a-day. My kickboxing was upped to 45 minutes and I was doing 50 push-ups at the end of every workout. My calorie intake was dropped dramatically and all carbs and fat were cut from my diet. I was sustaining on chicken and lettuce, and I really saw results. I was tanning every day and increasing my water intake to a gallon per day.

I was very careful not to dehydrate, because that would be a huge setback that I couldn't risk.

The hardest part now would be writing my acceptance speech. I had tried to write it when I first got the call, but I had no idea how to start it. Or finish it. Or write the middle.

See, it is very easy for me to be Sunny, and ramble in character on the microphone for ten minutes. But I've never had to be myself—be Tamara—and speak from the heart. I found this to be incredibly scary and difficult to do.

Then I thought to myself, when I cut a promo in character, I'm basically telling a story. So when I get on that stage, why don't I just tell my story—the story of becoming Sunny.

When I realized that, writing my speech became

second nature. The words seemed to flow onto paper so easily. My writer's block was gone, and I now had my speech written and ready to deliver to the world.

On March 31, 2011, John and I made our way, in first class, down to Atlanta, Georgia, home to WrestleMania XXVII. A stretch limo picked us up at the airport and delivered us to the host hotel. We checked into the green room and I picked up my itinerary to see what appearances I was scheduled for at Axxess throughout the weekend. The weekend of my life had officially begun.

I had never been so busy in my entire life. Between appearances at Axxess, a media day with the Rock, rehearsals, cocktail parties, the gym, tanning, and squeezing in small meals when I could, I may have had four hours of sleep each night. If not for the adrenaline and excitement of what was to come to me that Saturday night, I would have collapsed from exhaustion.

Finally, the day had come. The Hall of Fame ceremony was that evening, the night before WrestleMania. The butterflies in my stomach had grown into Mothras and and my anxiety was through the roof. I sat in my hotel room that morning and I looked back over my entire life to that point. I had succeeded in every job I had ever been given. I made history over and over again in my industry. I lived through three incredibly trying times in my life when I lost Daddy, Stacey, and Christopher.

I came back from the brink of death with my pancreatitis.

I had persevered.

And tonight was my reward.

When I arrived at the arena, I got into hair and make-up, rehearsed my speech one more time, and put on my gorgeous red gown.

Then it was showtime!

Backstage, we had to be photographed and filmed with Vince McMahon presenting us with our rings.

Always the ham, I thought of a way to make Vince laugh on camera, like I had always done in the past. As I walked up to him and put my hand out, he placed my Hall of Fame ring on my finger, and I said, "Yes, I'll marry you!"

The entire room, including Vince, erupted in laughter.

The clock was ticking and I waited my turn to walk on that stage and claim what was mine. I knew my speech from start to finish, every last word, but I jotted down notes on some cards, just in case.

Then, it was finally time. Thirteen Divas walked passed me to join my presenters, Michelle McCool and Layla, on stage.

My chest tightened and my hands shook.

They showed a compilation video on the giant screen overhead, to educate the 12,000 in attendance and the millions who would be watching at home, of my accomplishments throughout the years.

LayCool then began their introduction speech. I have to admit, I had wanted Trish Stratus to induct me, but I didn't have a choice in the matter as most inductees do.

Then, it was time. It was finally time. I was standing at the curtain waiting to hear my introduction and theme music when, all of a sudden, I couldn't remember my speech! Not a single word of it! Not

202

how it started, not how it finished, and definitely nothing in the middle!

I started freaking out in my own head. I felt sweat beads forming on my forehead and nose. I felt the clamminess overcome my palms.

Shit! I was going to totally fuck up my once-in-a-lifetime moment!

Then I reminded myself—just tell your story.

I never rehearsed or planned out any promos in the past, so why should I start now? I needed to calm down and have confidence in my abilities.

My music hit. They said my name. I took a deep breath, and out I walked.

I walked out on stage to a standing ovation, careful to not snag my six-inch stiletto platform heels on the carpet and fall ever-so-gracefully flat on my face. As I approached the podium, the applause got louder, and I basked in the crowd admiration for a few moments.

"This is it," I thought. "Your turn to shine. Just breathe, relax, and do what you do best. Tell your story."

Many people said that what followed over the next 15 minutes was the best speech of the night. I didn't ramble, I didn't stutter, I didn't slur, I didn't forget anything or anyone.

I told my story.

And what a story it was.

That night, April 3, 2011, was truly amazing and life-changing for me.

I achieved something that 98% of professional wrestlers only dream of achieving.

I worked so diligently at my craft for more than

21 years and the WWE Universe, and the world finally recognized it.

I was inducted along with Shawn Michaels, the Road Warriors, Hacksaw Jim Duggan, Bob Armstrong, Abdullah the Butcher, and comedian Drew Carey (who was inducted as a celebrity guest).

It was ironic to be inducted with Shawn, wasn't it? When we took group photos, Shawn and I were in the middle, facing each other. They almost looked like wedding party photos, with us as the bride and groom and the other inductees as the groomsmen! Ha! The irony!

The entire weekend was truly magical, a once in a lifetime experience.

It was an experience I'll never forget.

CHAPTER 27
I'LL HAVE THE ALL-YOU-CAN -EAT RIBS, PLEASE?

Ribs: Definition (1) n. The set of bones surrounding the chest cavity protecting the lungs and heart. (2) n. A tasty dish served at barbeque restaurants. (3) n. A prank pulled amongst bored, restless professional wrestlers for amusement and to break up the monotony of being on the road, often resulting in the embarrassment of the recipient.

For this chapter, we are going with definition number three.

The road can get crazy and monotonous and boring at the same time. When 30 or more wrestlers are together, day in and day out, for weeks on end, not only do they get tired of looking at each other, but they also need to do something to pass the time.

This is when the rib comes into play.

Most of the time, ribs are humorous and pulled between friends, mostly for the amusement and humiliation of the victim, but the ribs can be cruel, and often are.

I wasn't sure where to put the stories that are in this chapter throughout the book, so I decided they deserved a chapter all their own. Whenever I do an interview or talk to fans, I always seem to get asked about the best ribs I've seen over the years. The following is a compilation of hilarious ribs, little known facts, and unbelievable stories I have experienced on the road.

Enjoy! And read with caution...

* * *

The very first rib that was pulled on me in the WWF was by the master of ribs, Mr. Fuji. Fuji was well-known and feared for his ribs because his weren't always just fun and games. It wasn't uncommon for him to cause harm to someone.

I had just begun on the road as Sunny, and I made sure I was cordial and respectful to everyone in the locker room, especially the old-timers.

Mr. Fuji had the nightly job of braiding Yokozuna's hair. But this one night, as I was walking by them, he stopped me and asked me to braid Yoko's hair, because Fuji had a promo to shoot. Of course I wasn't going to say no to Mr. Fuji, so I walked behind Yoko and started combing and braiding. The seamstresses, who were right next to me, started laughing, but I didn't know why. Then Mr. Fuji walked by us, and laughed. Again, I had no idea why.

Then I smelled something foul, but I didn't know what it was

I realized what it was: YOKO'S HAIR!

His hair reeked like shit and sewage! He was so obese that he couldn't raise his hands over his head to wash his hair, and it was pungent!

When I was done, I ran to my locker room to wash my hands, but I couldn't get the stink off of them. It took three days for my hands to finally be Yoko-free. That's why everyone was laughing.

Mr. Fuji 1—Sunny 0.

* * *

One afternoon, I was walking in the backstage hallway when I came upon Jeff Jarrett and Hunter Hearst Helmsley talking. I stopped, looked at them both, and said, "Double J... Triple H... Double J... Triple H!"

That became my nickname for him from then on. Soon, Shawn was calling him Triple-H. Then the rest of the Clique caught on. Before you knew it, he was being introduced as Triple-H, and the name stuck.

Now everyone knows him as Triple-H, and probably 70% of wrestling fans today wouldn't know who Hunter Hearst Helmsley was if their life depended on it.

Yep, I gave Triple-H his name. Will I ever get credit for it? Probably not.

* * *

I "financially supported" "Stone Cold" Steve Austin and The Rock when they first started with the WWE by paying for their meals on a regular basis.

* * *

The USWA "borrowed" me from the WWE on a few occasions to work their Memphis TV tapings on Saturday morning. Instead of a hotel, I stayed at Casa de Lawler, at the urging of his then-wife Stacy. His house was very, very nice inside, especially the Coca-Cola room! It was a room off the kitchen completely decorated with Coca-Cola memorabilia. He had everything from a Coca-Cola jukebox to Coca-Cola straw and napkin dispensers! It was very cool.

* * *

The Kings of Ribs were undoubtedly Owen Hart and Davey Boy Smith. I was often either the victim of them or a willing participant.

On a month long tour of Germany, we rode on a tour bus from city to city around the country. There was a tiny bathroom down a skinny set on stairs on the bus that I noticed none of the boys used. I figured it was because of the horrible stench the tiny latrine had, but I couldn't pee in a bottle like most of the boys.

So on long ten hour rides, I had to go into it, because we didn't stop often enough at rest stops. On this one long trip, I snuck down into the bathroom while everyone was asleep.

When I was through, I put my hand on the door handle and pushed the door. It didn't move. I pushed and pushed and pushed and pushed. It finally opened an inch. I peeked out and saw the whole stairway was blocked with every single suitcase that was on board! Somebody had barricaded me into the tiny, smelly, pee-covered bathroom.

And I wasn't just in there for a few minutes; I was locked in there for two hours.

I tried to bang on the door and push my way out, but to no avail.

Then I heard a laugh. A very distinct, British laugh. The culprit was Davey Boy, the British Bulldog.

If he and I weren't such good friends, I might have been pissed off, but I knew it was all in good fun.

* * *

Owen Hart had a reputation for being one of the cheapest guys on the road. He would spend the least amount of money possible and get as much for free as he could.

On that same trip to Germany, we had a free full breakfast every day in our hotels. Owen took advantage of the free food and drink and filled his two duffel bags with pastries, bagels, and a quart of orange juice in each bag.

That's all Owen would travel with, two small duffel bags, so he wouldn't have to check any luggage. He would just carry them on.

Davey Boy knew this, and that was a huge mistake.

When we arrived at the airport and went to the desk to check in, Owen was first in line. The desk attendant asked if he had any bags to check, and he said no. Then Davey, who was right behind him, chimed in.

"I'm sorry ma'am, but those bags are too big to carry on," Davey chirped. "He'll have to check them."

"Shut up, Davey," Owen muttered out of the corner of his mouth. "I always carry these on."

The desk attendant took another look at Owen's carry-on bags. "Oh, I'm sorry sir, but they do look too big. I'll be happy to check them for you."

She took his bags and put them on the conveyor belt.

Owen was furious. He knew what was going to happen.

When we arrived at our next city, we proceeded to the baggage claim belt. As the bags started coming out, we all saw Owen's two little duffel bags leaking orange juice out of every seam and running down the belt!

All of his clothes were stained with orange, his regular clothes and his gear. That's what Owen got for sneaking O.J. in his bags.

It was all too funny. Davey and Owen used to battle with one another over ribs. They were the champs.

* * *

Sometime in 2000, Chris, Sabu and I were booked on a two-week tour of Australia. It was my first trip there. so I was very excited.

After a long 22-hour flight, we were in line at customs. Chris and I got through fine, but they decided to search Sabu.

They confiscated all of Sabu's many pills. He was furious. When we got to our hotel, we were exhausted. Chris and I decided to order some food to our room.

When I looked at the phone, I was confused. Besides the number buttons, there were three buttons to the side of them. They were labeled:

Room Service
Massage
Doctor

210

Room Service, Massage, and Doctor, oh my! What in the world were these for?

So I pressed the Room Service button, and ordered some dinner. Then I pressed "massage," and after about 20 minutes, two masseuses came up with portable tables. Then we pressed "Doctor." Thirty minutes later, a doctor came to our room with a tackle box. He set it upon the bed, opened it up, and asked, in his thick Australian accent, "So, what were you looking for?"

He had everything.

Vicodin, Soma, Percocet, Demerol, Xanax, Valium, Clenbuterol, and various steroids. Of course, he also had antibiotics and antihistamines, but we weren't really interested in that.

It cost $40 for a prescription, and he filled it right there. The best thing was, there was no limit!

So we called Sabu the next day and told him to come to our room.

I pressed the buttons. All three of them.

Sabu was amazed when we got our food with a side of massages and prescription pills to wash it down!

Ha! This obviously became our daily ritual.

Room Service, Massage, and Doctor... Oh my!

No wonder none of us could remember much of that two-week tour!

* * *

In 1997, Marc Mero needed knee surgery. When he was off the road, his wife, Sable, traveled with Ken Shamrock.

211

We all soon found out that they were doing much more than "travelling" together …

* * *

Speaking of Sable, in the WWF, she used to talk about how she and Kimberly were such good friends. Come to find out, they knew each other long before their wrestling involvement from their days as strippers at the Gold Club in Atlanta.

Who would'a thunk it?

* * *

Chris and I were traveling with Lex Luger and Davey Boy Smith in Vermont. Davey was driving and, in towns in Vermont, the roads are up and down hills with traffic lights at the bottom of each hill.

The roads were pretty icy and Davey was driving pretty fast, so he blew through one, two, three, four red lights in a row!

Of course, he got pulled over by a cop. The cop said, "Sir, you just ran four red lights in a row!" in an angry voice.

Davey replied, in his heavy British accent, "Oh, I'm sorry sir, but I'm from England. And in England, red means go."

The cop got flustered.

"Well, alright sir, but just so you know, in the United States, red means stop and green means go. Now be careful and have a nice day."

Ha! And we drove away, ticket free.

Davey could convince anyone of anything.

* * *

In Germany, we had one afternoon off in West Berlin. Chris and I had a craving for McDonald's, so we hailed a cab and they took us to a McDonald's in a mall. It was kind of a long ride, so the cabbie gave us a business card with the phone number to call them to be picked back up.

We ate, walked around the mall, and gave them a call. The cab dispatcher only spoke German, so we asked everyone we saw if they spoke English. One lady stopped to help. She got on the phone, spoke some German, and hung up.

She said we were somewhere in East Germany, and the cab we called doesn't come out that far.

Doesn't come out that far? But they brought us here, and we don't even know where we were!

She told us to go up to the bus stop and catch a bus. So we walked up to the bus stop on the side of a busy street, but the bus route map was all in German. We didn't know where we were, but we knew we were far from the hotel ... and we didn't even know the name of the hotel. It was 4:00 p.m. and our tour bus would be leaving for the show at 5:00 p.m. We were never going to make it back. I broke down and sat on the curb and cried.

Fuck! We were lost in East Berlin, with no way of getting back to our hotel, wherever that was!

We sat there hopeless and crying for about ten minutes, when suddenly, we heard something in the distance. Could it be? Could it be the WWF wrestling theme song album?

Yep, we heard the faint sounds of Bret Hart's

213

theme song. Then the song became louder and louder. One of the cars in the traffic jam in front of us must be playing it.

Finally a car rode up, and started yelling at us. It was a small car, with four girls wearing Bret Hart T-shirts playing his music. Chris and I looked at each other and, without hesitation, ran up to the car, swung open the door, and dove in.

We were saved!

The girls knew a little English, but they were on their way to the show, and they knew the hotel where we were staying.

After signing a few autographs and taking some pictures, the girls graciously dropped us off at the hotel just in time for us to get on the bus and head to the show.

My eyes were a swollen mess from crying, but we were saved!

Note to self: *Don't* get in a strange cab in a strange country just because you're jones-ing for a Big Mac!!

* * *

I was the first wrestling personality besides Hulk Hogan to be featured on mainstream television programs such as *Entertainment Tonight, Extra, Access Hollywood, Inside Edition, MTV's Singled Out,* and *MTV's Oddville.*

I was often referred to as "the female Hulk Hogan" due to my overwhelming popularity.

* * *

In 1996, at the WWF Slammy Awards, I was awarded the "Best Buns" and "Minds Behind the Mayhem" Awards.

* * *

I was the first, and only, manager in WWE history to be the manager of three consecutive sets of tag team champions.

* * *

The brand new Gund Arena in Cleveland, Ohio, had just opened, and the WWF was the first live event to be held there. This arena was beautiful. The locker rooms were spacious and carpeted wall-to-wall. Even the walls themselves were carpeted.

I noticed Bret standing by a table looking down at it. I walked over to see that there was a sheet cake on the table with Bret's picture airbrushed on it, and it was a very good likeness.

"Are you going to eat that?" I asked Bret.

He said no, that it had come from a fan, and he walked away.

A few minutes later, I saw Davey Boy standing by the cake. He called me over.

"Tammy, smell the nose. It smells like strawberry," he said.

Now, if it was anyone other than Davey, I may have smelled the nose. But there was no way in hell I was putting my face near that cake with him standing right there. So I thought I'd beat him at his own game.

I stuck my hand deep in the center of the cake,

lifted a good-sized chunk out, and smashed it right in Davey's face, on his glasses and all.

He paused in shock, and as the cake fell from his face. "Oh, OK, Tammy," he said, as he regained his composure. "Shit's on now!"

He picked up the entire sheet cake and chased after me down the long, carpeted locker room hallway. When I reached the end with nowhere to go, I felt a huge mound of cake splatter on the back of my head. When I turned around, Davey was standing next to Owen, who had just come out of the locker room to see what we were up to.

Davey and I made eye contact. He gave me a wink, and the entire cake went up into Owen's face with such force that the back of his head hit the wall behind him.

Owen slid the sheet cake down off of his frosting-covered face, into his arms.

"OK, Davey," he said. He walked back into the locker room and dumped the entire cake into Davey's gear bag, making his trunks a sweaty-smelling dessert.

At this point, the entire locker room was cracking up, including me, who was peering into the doorway, at Davey's misfortune. Davey saw me and yelled, "Tammy, you think that's funny, huh?"

I ran for my life down the hallway with Davey hot on my trail. I ran into my locker room, another dead end, and passed Chris who was sitting in a chair, completely unaware of what was going on out in the hallway.

Davey and I were at a stand-off, with our hands full of cake and icing, prepared for a duel. Only this time, Chris was sitting in the middle.

Davey and I locked eyes again, winked, and we instantly knew we were on the same wavelength. At the same time, we turned and our handfuls of cake went flying at Chris' face, exploding all over the carpeted wall behind him.

Just at that very moment, our road agent, Tony Garea, walked in.

"What is this travesty?" he screamed. Davey and I scurried out of the room leaving Chris to take the brunt of Tony's scolding, even though he was just an innocent bystander.

When it was all said and done, the brand spanking new carpeted walls and floors of the Cleveland Gund Arena were covered with buttercream icing.

Davey and I were each fined $500 and we were made to stay after the show and clean the carpets with wet towels.

It was absolutely hilarious as we were scrubbing the walls, still covered from head to toe in cake. It was the best $500 each of us had ever spent.

* * *

Percy Pringle (Paul Bearer) passed away as I was writing this memoir. The news of his death made me think of a rib the boys used to play, not on him, but on his son.

His son was about seven or eight years old at the time; a roly-poly freckle-faced redhead who would come to shows often with his dad.

One particular show, the boys really did a number on the kid.

217

They hoisted him up to the ceiling and pressed his back against the metal air conditioning duct running across the ceiling. The Undertaker and Kane, the tallest guys on the bunch, taped him to the duct with duct tape.

Around and around, over and over, until he was strapped to the ceiling by his waist, with his arms and legs flailing in the air!

The kicker was that the boys left him there for the entire length of the show! Three hours!

When Percy walked in, looked up, and saw his son strung up like a bug on a spider web, he just laughed a big belly laugh and left him there.

You'd think the boy would never come back to a show because of this, but he was a glutton for punishment. And every time he came back, he was taped up to the ceiling again!

* * *

Every time we were booked in Canada, we dreaded the trip. It was boring, had bad food, and was full of ice-covered towns.

This tour, we were going to be on the road for two weeks straight, all across Ontario and Quebec.

We all decided to chip in on a 12-passenger van to save on rental, gas and toll money. There were nine of us: me, Chris, Davey Boy, Billy Gunn, Bart Gunn, Goldust, Marty Jannetty, Al Snow, and Owen Hart.

In the first couple days of our tour, Owen rode with us, but then jumped in a van with a fan, which he did quite often. Owen was the cheapest man alive, so anywhere he could save a buck, he did.

So the eight of us were riding in our brand new, white Ford 12-passenger van, with Al Snow at the wheel, and Owen driving the fan's van right behind us on the QEW.

The QEW is a long highway spanning the width of Ontario past Toronto, through Quebec, up to Montreal. It's about eight lanes wide, so there is quite a bit of traffic on the expressway.

There is nothing to see along this highway except the slew of gas stations, truck stops, and Tim Horton's coffee shops dotting the side of the road.

As we quickly approached one truck stop, we noticed a sign that read, "Fireworks on sale here!"

What? Fireworks? For sale legally at a truck stop? We just had to check this out.

We stopped to grab a bite to eat and check out what explosives were available.

We did our shopping and piled back in our van. We had rockets, Roman candles, stink bombs, smoke bombs, and sparklers. We were set. But we were on a four-hour drive into Quebec. What were we to do with them?

Marty Jannetty was riding in the front passenger seat, so he acted as the DJ for our trip. He popped in a cassette tape of the soundtrack for the movie *Dangerous Minds*, the Michelle Pfeiffer movie featuring Coolio's song, "Gangsta's Paradise." This tape got everybody a little pumped up, especially Goldust, Marty, and Davey, who started an impromptu wrestling match in one of the middle seats.

They were rocking so feverishly back and forth on this middle bench seat that the bolts ripped right out of the floor. What were we to do with a dislodged middle bench seat? Well, what any bunch of responsible, grown men would do, naturally—open up the side door and toss it out onto the highway at 80 miles per hour!

Oh my God! I couldn't believe they just threw out the seat! There were lots of other cars on the road, and they just opened the door and threw it out.

We were driving in the middle of a blizzard, and there were already two feet or so of snow on the ground. Marty opened the front passenger side window to allow the blizzard to coat the inside of the van white. It was an old-fashioned manual crank window, so when it was all the way down, Marty broke the handle.

Why did he break it? Because it was there.

What were the repercussions? We couldn't close the window in the middle of a blizzard.

Then came the fun part. We realized we had bought all those fireworks!

Owen was still behind us, so Davey thought of a great way to rib him and the fan. We opened all the side windows of the van and armed ourselves with rockets and Roman candles.

Upon Davey's orders, we lit them all, and shot balls of fire out of the van directly at Owen behind us.

Owen caught on to what we were doing, so he strategically placed himself right behind us to catch the multi-colored fireballs in the grill of the van he was driving.

We all died in laughter as the fan's van began filling up with smoke, almost to where you couldn't see their faces through the windows.

Our adrenaline was so fired up, that we lit our

multi-colored smoke bombs in our van, until the interior looked like a psychedelic kaleidoscope.

Our fun came to an end when we arrived at the venue.

The next few days we spent on the road in this completely trashed van with no middle seat, burns in the carpet, and a passenger front window that was permanently down.

When it was time to return the van, Davey Boy confronted the rental agent, addressing him in his strong, convincing British accent.

"I can't believe you rented me a van in this condition! The front window is broken, there is no middle seat, and it smells of smoke with burns all over the carpet! I had my wife and children in this van! This is a travesty!

The rental agent was so embarrassed and convinced that the van was rented out in this condition that he refunded the two weeks rental onto Davey's credit card and gave him a free week's rental.

Davey walked away laughing and smiling with pride at his accomplishment.

Why? Because the funniest part was that he wasn't even the original rental! It wasn't rented on his credit card, but he got it refunded to him. He turned a profit on the deal!

Ha! Oh, that crazy Davey Boy.

* * *

When I was a kid, meeting my favorite wrestlers at the Howard Johnson's, we became familiar faces since we were there every month. One night, as Paul

Orndorff was leaving for the gym, he walked up to my sister and me and said, "Hey girls, I hate to bother you, but can you do me a favor? I forgot to wash my wrestling gear for tonight and I'm headed to the gym now. Can you wash and dry it for me so it'll be clean for tonight?"

We quickly answered. "Of course!"

So we had the honor of washing Mr. Wonderful's trunks and kneepads!

We were tempted to walk off with them, but then that would probably have ruined our autograph and picture taking at the Newark Ho-Jo's!

* * *

In 1999 and 2000, I was doing some fitness modeling for bodybuilding magazines. All of my photo shoots were in Venice, California, so I would shoot out there when I went for TV and movie auditions.

One of my photographers, Rick Schaff, was a really nice guy, and well known in the bodybuilding world.

We were out on Main St. in Venice doing a shoot along a waterway that had some nautical pilings in tall green grass. I was wearing a one-piece bathing suit that barely covered more than a bikini.

My skin was tanned and glistening with baby oil and sweat, and my poses were rather, shall we say, *provocative* in nature.

We were getting plenty of honks and catcalls from all the cars passing by and a few pedestrians stopped for a few minutes to watch the session.

Down the sidewalk, we saw a rollerblader headed our way. His eyes were on me, and not on the sidewalk in front of him, where they should have been.

As he passed by, he was looking over his shoulder at me, his neck twisted and contorted to what must have been a painful position.

We turned our attention away from him and all of a sudden we heard a man screaming in pain!

We looked back, and saw the rollerblader lying on the ground, holding his leg and yelling in agony. We called 911 from our cell phone, and Rick ran over to him to see if he was OK.

It just so happened that as he was paying more attention to my near-naked body than the sidewalk, his skate caught on a large crack and he went tumbling down to the ground, and he broke his lower leg in the process!

So I can now say that my sexy good looks not only broke men's hearts, but their limbs as well!

CHAPTER 28
OVER BARBED WIRE AND THROUGH THE WOODS, TO THE LIQUOR STORE WE GO!

After my Hall of Fame induction, things began to deteriorate between John and me. I won't go into any details because what happened is personal, and we remain good friends to this day.

After nearly six years together, we split in September of 2011. I had just come home from my first attempt at rehab, something I didn't want to do, but something I did upon his insistence. He thought I was drinking more than I was and gave me an ultimatum, so I called the WWE for treatment for the first time and went to Hazelden in Minnesota.

This attempt at rehab was not successful, and I was drunk there almost the entire time.

How was I drunk? Let's just say I became a master escape artist.

Since I didn't want to be there, I wanted to drink. On my way into rehab in the limo provided by the WWE, I noticed a small liquor store in the little town outside of Hazelden's grounds. I knew I could find my way there if I was sneaky enough.

There were security guards at the one entrance

and exit to the grounds, so I couldn't go out that way. I had to find a shortcut or something.

There was a long circular walking trail that went all around the facility, and I knew a part of it went out near the main road.

So I walked on the trail to a point where I thought I was parallel with the road and jumped through the four-foot high sticker bushes into the woods. I walked about 200 yards through the woods, under broken tree branches and around tree stumps, until I came to a four-foot high barbed wire fence. With the caution of a ninja, I climbed the fence and leapt to the ground on the other side.

I then walked through two residential backyards and up someone's long driveway to the main road. I made a left and about a quarter-mile down the road was the greatest discovery of all, the small mom and pop liquor store.

I bought my bottle of Southern Comfort, stashed it in my Victoria's Secret tote bag, and headed back the same way.

Down the road. Down the driveway. Through the backyards. Over the barbed wire fence. Through the 200 yards of woods. Through the sticker bushes. And back to the walking trail to the dorms.

Ha! I was good.

I took this journey every day for 15 days. I was drunk the entire time I was there.

At the two-and-a-half week mark, I decided to leave treatment. As I was packing up my things, I pulled the bottle of SoCo out of the personal safe in my room and said, "See! Your stupid rehab doesn't work!"

I've always said that when there's a will, there's a way, and rules were meant to be broken.

Poor Hazelden Treatment Center. They never saw me coming.

When I came home, I got my very own apartment for the first time in my life, on the beach in Long Branch, New Jersey.

Being alone for the first time in my life was complicated, and I didn't handle it well. My drinking spiraled out of control. All I cared about was drinking, and how I was going to acquire my next drink.

It was a very dark time in my life. I felt very alone.

I was so sick from drinking that I spent Thanksgiving, my birthday, Christmas, and New Year's Eve alone at home, drunk on my couch.

There were nights I wanted to die. I didn't want to kill myself; I wasn't suicidal. But I damned sure didn't want to wake up in the morning.

I function a lot better when I have someone to take care of, but when I'm alone, I can't even take care of myself.

I didn't have the tools or emotional stability to be a "single" person living alone.

Things were really bad. My health was suffering. I had a viral infection for six weeks, and then I spent a week in the hospital with a very low, very dangerous, low platelet count.

All of these illnesses were aggravated by my drinking.

Something had to change.

Something had to give.

CHAPTER 29
THE DEVIL'S SON

Damien.

Son of Lucifer.

Spawn of Satan.

From Day One, I should have known that name was a bad omen.

I should have run my fingers through his long curly hair to search for the number of the beast etched into his scalp.

My friends even joked about that name when they first heard of my new boyfriend.

It was mid-May, 2012, and my friend Tracii, who spent more time at my beachfront apartment than her own home, was telling me about a guy who was dying to meet me. He was younger, 26, and a wrestler on the indie scene for four years. I had never heard of him or met him at any shows, even though he was from Staten Island and I was from Jersey. We just never crossed paths.

So after some begging and pleading on his part, Tracii finally told me about him, and I looked him up on Facebook. She was going on and on about what a great guy he was, how much fun he was, blah, blah, blah, so I figured I'd check him out. At first look, I thought he was cute, but completely not my type. I wasn't into guys with long hair, I didn't want to get involved with another wrestler, and he, by her definition, was a "partier," which was not something that interested me. Yes, I was an alcoholic, but I've never been into the drug scene, so I was a little turned off by that.

But I "friended" him on Facebook anyway, and we started chatting, then we exchanged numbers. We started texting, then talking. A lot. Every night. For five hours a night. For five nights straight.

The first night we were finding so much we had in common. By the second night we were finishing each other's sentences. By the fifth night, I turned to Tracii and said, "I think I'm in love with this guy!"

He was definitely quick-witted, and extremely charming, and he won me over fast. He was constantly complimenting me, and singing to me on the phone, since I found out he used to sing in a rock cover band.

But he still wasn't my type. I'm into sports, especially MMA. He hated all sports.

I wanted to be a doctor. He had to go to summer school in high school. He was really into music and fashion. I was stuck in the 80's and loved my sweatpants.

On that fifth night of talking, a Thursday night, he asked if I wanted to go out the following night. I told him that I would have liked to, but I already had dinner plans with a guy named Adam whom I had already cancelled on once before. He was begging me to cancel on him again, but I said I couldn't do it, that it would be too mean. So our call ended at 2:00 a.m., and I went to sleep.

By 9:00 a.m. the next morning, I cancelled my date with Adam, *again*, and texted D and said that I was all his that night. I told him we'd use the dinner reservations I already had, but to bring his toothbrush, just in case.

So D got out of work around 5:30 p.m. and headed down for our dinner reservations at 8:30. We had forgotten that it was Memorial Day weekend, so the highways were packed. He didn't get down to my place until 8:15 and he still had to shower before dinner.

He called me as he was coming up my street, Melrose Terrace, so I told him I'd meet him downstairs in the parking garage because I had to get him a guest parking pass.

As I was walking into the entrance of the garage, I just so happened to turn around, and at that moment I saw silver Nissan Maxima turn into the garage. Through the glare on the windshield I could make out a man with curly hair pulled back into a ponytail. Our eyes met, and I knew it was him. I turned around, walked up to his car; got in, reached across the dozen roses he had for me, grabbed him by the back of the head, and kissed him.

No "hi." No "hello." No "how was your drive?" I just kissed him. Hard.

It was instantaneous, love at first sight. I was dressed and all done up, he was sweaty and dirty from work, but that made him even sexier. His scent was undeniably sexy. There are such things as pheromones, and my sexual radar was definitely picking up on his.

So we parked the car and headed up the elevator to apartment 414, my place. We went in, he pushed me up against the wall, and we made out, for about ten

229

minutes. Finally I pushed him off and made him get in the shower, since now we were already late for our reservations.

When he was done, he stepped out of the shower, fully naked. No shame. I had an exhibitionist on my hands. He had nothing to be ashamed of. A beautiful body—a little thin for my usual taste—and a very attractive penis. And probably the best butt I had seen in a long time. He definitely wasn't shy about being in his birthday suit, but then again, neither am I.

He finally put on some clothes, looked fantastic, more fashionable than me, and we went to dinner. Throughout the meal, he was holding my hand, and kept getting out of his chair to come over and kiss me. A total romantic, I was falling in love fast.

After dinner, we speed-walked back across the street to my apartment, flew up the stairs, and before we knew it, we were tearing each other's clothes off and were engaged in the most sensual, passionate sex session that I have had in a long time. Everything was perfect. Every movement, every thrust, every kiss, every drop of sweat from his chest that landed on my tongue—perfect.

That night we stayed up until around 8:00 a.m. making love, over and over again.

The next day, he was supposed to go to two Memorial Day barbeques, but he cancelled them both. What was to be a dinner date had now turned into a four-day weekend of sex, debauchery, and more sex. The only time we left the bedroom was to use the bathroom or go to the door for our food delivery. For four straight days. Unreal. By the third day, we were both so sore, but we kept going.

On Monday, we both didn't want him to leave, but he got called in to work, so we kissed goodbye and made plans for the following weekend.

I was in love. Undeniably and completely in love, and so was he.

The next few weekends went exactly like the first. After work on a Thursday or Friday, he'd drive the two and a half hours down from Connecticut to spend the weekend with me.

We went out, we cooked, we went to the beach, and we made love—a lot. Everything was falling into place beautifully.

Until…

… During a mid-week phone call, he said he needed to tell me something. OK, here we go. What is it? He hesitantly tells me he has a roommate. Fine, no big deal. The roommate is his ex-girlfriend. OK. Really big deal!

"Are you kidding me?" I said upset, angry and stunned.

He explained to me that he'd been trying to get her to move out for months and that she wouldn't leave and had nowhere to go. Blah, blah, blah.

I was stunned, confused, mortified. I was pissed the fuck off!

This should have been the red flag of all red flags, but I brushed it off as him being too nice a guy to toss someone out on the street.

I tried to deal with it the best I could, but my best turned out to be drinking more and more heavily, each and every day, morning until night. I would binge for four or five days straight with little food or water.

The pattern turned out to be, when he was with

me on weekends I hardly drank. I was happy. When he was home with her during the week, I drank like a fish. When I think about it, I guess it was my way of coping with the thoughts of him sharing an apartment with her, and me having to trust and believe that nothing sexual was going on.

Needless to say, it was driving me absolutely insane to the point where I might as well have had an intravenous drip of vodka 24-hours a day.

I just couldn't handle it. I wanted to believe that it was over between them, but I couldn't do it sober. So I drank. And drank. To the point where I ended up back in the hospital a few times.

One time I woke up in the hospital and saw him sitting next to me. He had arrived at my place on his usual Thursday night and found me unresponsive. I had a blood alcohol level of .540. They told me a .40 was considered fatal. How the hell was I alive?

That was when D and I sat down and decided it was time for me to go to rehab. I couldn't live like that anymore. I couldn't be the drunken lush that did nothing but lay on the couch 24 hours a day all week long with a bottle of vodka in my hand and a dozen empties lying around me on the floor. It got to the point where I wouldn't even get off the couch to throw anything out, not empty bottles, not food, nothing.

I would live all week long on top of piles of trash and clean feverishly when D was on his weekly ride down to see me. The only time I saw my bed was with him. I was always too drunk or too sick from being drunk to get off the couch at all. I would go days without a shower. Days without brushing my teeth. THIS was my bottom.

But I could still muster up enough energy to make the three-block trip to the liquor store when I ran out.

Correction: I *never* ran out. I would always make sure I had enough to get me through the morning until the liquor store opened at 10:00 a.m. If I didn't, I'd drag myself off the couch, even in a thunderstorm, and get to the store at 9:59 p.m., right before they closed, because God forbid I woke up at 5:00 a.m. dry, and shaking from withdrawal.

The Pakistani owners of my friendly neighborhood booze shack knew me by name. They even let me take home bottles when I forgot my wallet, because I was too drunk to remember it on the way out. They always spotted me, because they knew I'd always be back for more.

I even had a cabbie named Jessie—nice older Hindu guy—on speed dial on my phone. On those days when I didn't feel like going to the store myself, he'd pick up a bottle and deliver it to me at my building. Convenient, huh?

This is what I had become. I was a drunken mess, no better than the homeless drunks sleeping in cardboard boxes under a bridge. The only difference is I had a place to sleep ... barely. I was more concerned with having enough booze cash than paying my $1,500 monthly rent. Twice I was given eviction notices and had to go to court to pay the back rent by the thousands to be able to stay.

This is what I had become, what I swore to myself I'd never become.

But I did.

CHAPTER 30
MORE LOBSTER, PLEASE?

I finally mustered up enough guts to pick up the phone and call Ann Russo, the head of the WWE Wellness Program Department. Let me tell you, this is NOT an easy phone call to make. Your whole body shakes as you dial. When she picks up, you have to fight the urge to not hang up, then comes the hard part.

"Hi Ann, it's Tammy. I think I need help. Again."

Whew! I did it. It's the hardest thing any alcoholic or addict will ever do, to ADMIT you need help.

See, all alcoholics and addicts are in the same mindset—denial. We all think our problem isn't that bad, we can control it, and we can stop on our own if we want to.

Bullshit!

Our problem is that bad, we can't control it, and we *can't* stop on our own! It's humanly impossible! (So all of you out there, quit fucking fooling yourselves, 'K?)

So Ann told me she'd make a few calls and get right back to me. Within two hours, I got the call saying there was a bed waiting for me at 9:00 a.m. the next morning at Silver Hill Hospital in New Canaan, Connecticut.

Here is where the fear sets in. Oh my fucking God. I'm going back in. What do I pack? I don't want to pack! I can't sleep. I can't go tomorrow! Oh my God. I'll try to stop on my own.

The fear and panic is almost too much to bear. There is no semblance of relief by thinking, "Ah, I'm going to get sober and feel much, much better." Nope. None of that happens. None.

All night long, I was freaking out, with D unsuccessfully trying to talk me down. Nothing worked. I was awake all night and decided to pack 20 minutes before we were supposed to leave for the place. Ugh. I was a mess, a complete and utter panicky mess.

I forced myself into the shower, and then we were off to rehab.

As we pulled up, I was delighted to see this beautiful country club setting, with beautiful horses, tennis courts, a pool and gym and happy people everywhere. We were greeted at admissions like we had just arrived at our resort for a lovely vacation. The dining room was staffed with four professional chefs who served us lobster two or three times a week. Seriously, lobster! Chef Henry, who became my close, personal friend, would grill me up some chicken breasts if the menu ever consisted of too many fried or saucy foods. The omelet station cook, Eddie, with his long dreadlocks and Bob Marley-like easy going attitude, wouldn't even need to ask how I wanted my omelet each morning—he knew. It was his job to know. I knew how to get the right people in my pocket, which I always did.

235

The house I lived in was gorgeous; hard wood floors, some single bedrooms, granite kitchen, leather sofas; just gorgeous.

OK, now that I'm done with the infomercial selling Silver Hill, I won't bore you with the details of what goes on at rehab, because you've probably read about it many times before.

But this is what it sums up to:

1) Groups
2) One-on-one sessions
3) More groups
4) AA and NA meetings
5) More groups
6) And the occasional "rehab romance" (not for me, though)

Another thing fantastic about SHH was that we had visiting hours every day. So D came four or five times a week to see me, and enjoyed Chef Henry's fine dining as well. Then he had me for dessert. Oh yeah, we shagged every time he came to visit.

My room was in a private upstairs corner of the house, so it was very easy to sneak away for 20 minutes or so.

My 33 days there came and went pretty quickly because of my posh accommodations, great cuisine, cool chicks as housemates, and seeing my Love almost every day.

On August 23, the day of my discharge, my Prince Charming (ahem) picked me up in his chariot and delivered me to my new home, his apartment in Branford, Connecticut.

When I walked through the door, I was in shock! Not a good shock, either. The place was a total pigsty.

As it turns out, the piece of shit ex-girlfriend didn't move out until the day before! Talk about last minute! She took everything! She didn't even leave him a roll of toilet paper! What she did leave was a giant mess for me to clean up!

I walked into the bathroom, and *oh my*—.

CHAPTER 31
HOME SWEET HOME ... OR SO I THOUGHT

The bathroom looked like it hadn't been cleaned in months! The kitchen, too! Filthy. Just filthy. Even in my most drunken states, I still managed to clean the bathroom and the kitchen once a week.

My belongings were already there in the storage unit beneath the apartment, but I couldn't possibly start unpacking until I had cleaned up this landfill first.

So Cinderella, I became. Scrubbing, washing, cleaning, more scrubbing, disinfecting, deodorizing (the place reeked of cat piss), and de-staining.

Wouldn't ya know it? The sink, toilet and tub really **weren't** all a lovely cream color! They were white! What a smashing discovery!

But I swallowed my pride and cleaned, trying not to make him feel bad in the process. After three days of hard labor we moved my things up from storage. We were finally making this place livable.

Everything was going fine, with the occasional coming across a picture of the witch that would totally set me off. We were trying to settle in and get used to living together, but this fucking bitch would not stop calling, texting, Facebooking or emailing him. Enough already! I put my foot down and told him he **had to** stop replying and cut ties, because of how uncomfortable it was making me.

I was doing great with my sobriety, and I didn't need anything, especially her, putting that in jeopardy. He promised he would, and we went on with life; going to the gym together, meeting his friends, going out to dinner with them, and doing the "Number One" no-no straight out of rehab: going to bars with him and his friends a few nights a week.

Big mistake. **Huge.**

I don't recommend this to a newly sober person at all.

Everything was going wonderfully for three and a half beautiful weeks. On Saturday night, September 11 (the date should have been another omen) we were all out at the local watering hole when D walked away from our table with a few of the guys. He left his cell phone with me ... Big mistake on his part.

He got a text message from HER asking, "Are you home?"

I figured I'd answer back as him and see what she wanted.

The conversation went like this:

Me (as D): "Why?"

Her: "Leave for a while."

Me: "For what?"

Her: "Let's fuck."

Me: "Why would I want to do that?"

Her: "Oh okay, don't act like we haven't been fucking."

With that, I stormed out of the bar to find him. I was bright red with rage and I was shaking

239

uncontrollably. I eventually found him in his car with the local drug dealer, snorting crushed Percocet 30's, which set me off even more. Like I said, I'm an alcoholic, not a drug addict. I pulled him out of the car and questioned him.

He was already high, so in his worst lying voice he tried to tell me that she was bullshitting to cause trouble. I made him call her and put her on speakerphone.

He accused her of making it up. She proceeded to describe their newly furniture-less friend Joe's apartment and how they had to fuck on a blanket on the floor. He just had a baffled look on his face as he was trying to convince me she was lying, but she knew too many details she shouldn't have known. And I'm not stupid.

By this time I was so furious and shaking with fear, rage, and betrayal, I wanted to knock his drugged-up ass out.

I stormed away and threatened to leave, and he pleaded with me to stay and to believe him that he didn't cheat on me. His furniture-less friend Joe even lied to my face for him.

Scumbag.

So stupid me gave him the benefit of the doubt and calmed down. The kicker of this entire sexual allegation was that it happened on August 31st, on **his birthday**, when I was home in the kitchen, making dinner for him, **in lingerie**, while he called and said he had to work an hour or two late that day. Really fucking nice, huh?

So Monday, while he was at work, what did I do? Relapse. I couldn't bear to think about him possibly

240

cheating on me just a week after I moved in with the bastard, so I drank. When he came home, we got into an argument about the allegations and me drinking, and he slapped me … So I hit him back! **Harder**. Then the MMA fighter in me came out and I put him in a guillotine chokehold. Yep, I choked his lying ass out.

When he came to, he immediately grabbed the phone and called 911. Subsequently, arrest number one.

CHAPTER 32
HOME AWAY FROM HOME—
THE BRANFORD POLICE DEPARTMENT AND
NEW HAVEN COURTHOUSE

I was arrested for "disorderly conduct." I had to spend the night on a cold metal cot in a dirty, dingy holding cell at the police station and go to court the next morning. In court, I was released on a "promise to appear" and a limited protective order was put in place. A limited PFA means I can return home, but can't argue, fight, harass, or stalk the "victim."

I went home and drank.

He came home. We argued.

He called the cops.

Here comes arrest number two; two arrests, two days in a row.

Another cold, dirty, lonely night in the police station holding cell, and back to court the next morning. Another "promise to appear," and now the PFA was raised to a full order of protection, which means I can't go home.

But where was I supposed to go? I lived there! I knew no one else in Connecticut besides his friends, and my family is in Jersey. So I went home. His parents were there and guess who else? The fucking bitch ex-girlfriend, sitting on my friggin' couch!

Son of a bitch!

D asked me to get in his car with him (he had stayed home from work) and we drove a couple blocks away and parked. He broke down and admitted to me that he did cheat on me with that pig.

I lost it. I got out, went to the liquor store, and walked home. We argued again and WHAM! Wouldn't ya' know it, he called the cops!

Arrest number three, three days in a row.

Back to the hell, I mean, the holding cell and court.

This time the SAME JUDGE looked at me and shook his head. This time my sister was in the courtroom, and pleaded for them to let me go home with her. They obliged, and she dropped me off at a diner so she could go to the apartment and get some of my things. She packed what she could, and we headed to Jersey.

While she was there packing, there was a news van and camera crews all over the apartment complex, getting interviews with neighbors. By now, my three arrests had made national headlines, were airing all over the 6:00 o'clock and 11:00 o'clock news on every channel across the New England area, and it even made it on Hollywood tabloid shows *TMZ* and *Dish Nation*.

Great. Just what I fucking needed. They had already been in the courtroom with a camera for all three arraignments, and now they were stalking the neighborhood. I arrived at my mom's house, spent a few days there, and prepared myself for my upcoming court-ordered ten-day stint in rehab at the Carrier Clinic in New Jersey.

By the time I went there, D and I were already speaking on the phone, and throughout my ten days there he pleaded and begged for forgiveness for what he had done—the cheating and the cop-calling. Because I'm a sucker and was in love with this asshole, I told him I would forgive him.

My logic was; since I was caught cheating in a past relationship, and wasn't forgiven, I knew how much it hurt and how much he must have been hurting. I didn't want to make the man I loved go through that emotional pain like I did, so I forgave him, and we agreed that I would come home to him when I got out.

He said he was so lonely, and couldn't stand spending one day without me, that he loved me more than anything ... Blah, blah, blah.

So I, the asshole, left that rehab, went back to my mother's, and waited for him to come pick me and my clothes up and head back "home" to Connecticut. On the ride, we had a long talk, and when we got home, we had an even longer talk—about how sorry we were, and how we were going to work it out, because we couldn't live without each other.

Okay.

Things were good for about a week, and we spent the weekend visiting his parents in Staten Island. On Sunday night, he told me that he got a text and phone call from work saying he had to go in for an emergency job at 10:30 p.m., that night. I was supposed to stay at his parents' house Sunday night and go into NYC on Monday for my outpatient treatment, but I told him I was going home with him that night and would commute to the city the next morning. I was suspicious, and he looked disgruntled.

So we drove home, and I sent him off to work. He texted at around midnight and said he'd be home around 1:00 or 1:30 a. m., earlier than he thought. Great! I waited up, he came home, and we went to bed.

The next morning, I wasn't feeling well, so I decided to skip my outpatient appointment and sleep in a little. I sent him off to work at 7:00 a.m., but couldn't fall back to sleep, so I figured I'd get online to see what was going on in the world.

Big mistake. **Huge!**

As I flipped open the laptop, his email popped on the screen, already logged in.

About eight emails down, past the junk mail, was an email from **you-know-who**!

Yep! Fucking whore! Son of a bitch!

Naturally, I opened it.

"It was great seeing you last night. I had fun. I can't believe I have a hickey—I feel like I'm 14! Ha-ha! I really missed you a lot, goodnight babe."

That was all I fucking needed to read.

I walked around the corner to you-know-where— the liquor store—with my cell phone in hand. I called him and in the most scared, angry, shaking voice screamed, "You did it to me again! Where did you go last night? Where were you last night?"

"I had to work, like I told you," he said. "Why?"

"Oh, yeah? Then what's this email from **her**? She has a hickey? She had fun last night? She missed you a lot? What the fuck?!"

He tried to calm me down. "Listen to me, it's not what you think," he said, trying to sound earnest and

245

genuine. "I did go to work, then she texted me to meet her at some bar she was at. I went, had a couple drinks. We talked, and I was only there for 15 minutes."

"You're a fucking liar! I can't believe you did this to me again! I'm gonna fuck the next guy I meet so you can see how it feels!"

I hung up on him, and guzzled from the liter-sized bottle of Svedka I had just purchased. My day went like this: drank, cried, ignored his calls and texts, drank, he came home, we argued, he called the cops.

Arrest number four.

Another violation of the full protective order. This is now my third violation.

Great.

Court the next morning was a little different. This time, they put a $25,000 surety bond on me, which meant I had to come up with ten percent and get a bondsman to get out. So I did. And the bondsman graciously drove me to the liquor store, then back home to our apartment, even though I wasn't supposed to be there.

When I got there, I realized I didn't have my keys. **Shit**. Now what? My cell phone was in the apartment, and I needed to get in, grab some clothes, and leave. Go to a hotel room, somewhere. He was at work, so I wanted to get in and out fast. I didn't want to see his face again.

So I did what all people naturally do when locked out of their homes. I scaled a wall and climbed up to the second floor balcony and went in through the sliding glass door. Yes, I'm a bit of a monkey.

I went in, grabbed a bag, my phone, and started packing some clothes, so I could get the fuck out.

Within five minutes, the cops were there! What the hell? He wasn't even home. We weren't even talking on the phone.

Well, a neighbor saw me climb the balcony and knew I wasn't supposed to be there, so he took it upon himself to call the cops! **Fuck me**!

Arrest number five.

This time, it was violation of the PFA and burglary (entering without a fucking key through the second floor balcony sliding glass door, even though it was my own apartment) and a $100,000 cash bond! That meant I needed $100,000 in cash to get out—no ten percent, no bondsman). I was fucked.

Since $100,000 cash is near impossible for **anyone** to come up with, I was carted off to jail. State prison, to be exact. Stuck there until my next court date, which was in 20 days. I was fucking terrified. In Connecticut, a Violation of a Protective Order is a five-year felony, and I now had four counts of it and a crappy public defender to boot.

Fuck my life.

CHAPTER 33
MIRACLES HAPPEN

*"John the Baptist, who was in prison, heard about all
the things the Messiah was doing. So he sent his
disciples to ask Jesus, 'Are you the Messiah we've
been expecting, or should we keep looking for
someone else?'"*—Matthew 11:23

I am now known as Inmate #393257.

I'm sitting in jail with three "bunkies."

Four miserable days go by—horrible food, a
lumpy mat to sleep on, lots of Gin Rummy played—
when they say I have a "professional visit."

Having no idea what or who it is, I head down to
the visitor's building.

I walk into the room, and there's some guy I've
never seen before sitting there in a sweater and jeans,
with a legal pad in front of him.

He introduces himself as Rob Serafinowicz—
attorney at law.

Hmmm.

He goes on to explain that he's friends with the
head legal counsel of the WWE, and saw my arrests on
the news and in the newspapers.

He wants to take on my case pro-bono.

I accepted the offer, but I wanted to know why he was interested in representing me, for free no less. As it turns out, Rob is a huge wrestling fan and—wouldn't ya' know it—a Sunny fan from the 90's.

Perfect, I thought. Now I have a Super Mark wanting to know all aspects of my life.

But that wasn't the case. He was highly intelligent, respectful, well-spoken, and didn't even discuss wrestling. He was just a former fan who wanted to help me out, because I didn't deserve to be in jail.

So on the eighth day in jail, a miracle happened. Rob got the judge to agree to send me to a long-term alcohol inpatient rehab instead of jail, and that when I was finished, I could withdraw my guilty plea to the PFA violations.

Fabulous! Three more months in rehab, but that was way better than jail.

After we left the courthouse together, and got through all the news cameras on the courthouse stairs just **dying** to get their story, we made our way to the nearest Burger King to get some sustenance in me. Yes, Burger King. Eight days in jail makes Burger King taste like filet mignon!

We then arrived at his office, where a black limo, courtesy of the WWE was waiting to pick me up and drive me out to Reading, Pennsylvania, a four and a half hour journey to the Caron Treatment Center.

On the car ride out, my phone buzzed with a text. It was D.

"Call me, now. Please."

I waited 20 minutes, and then called him.

"What do you want?"

249

He starts going on and on and crying, saying those were the worst eight days of his life, not hearing from me. He said he couldn't live without me. He said he downed a bottle of Xanax in one day trying to end his life from the thought of not having me.

I had heard all of this before … But I fell for it again … hook, line, and mother-fucking sinker.

I told him I still loved him after he professed his love for me, and I told him I'd call him later that night after I got settled in.

Long story short, he sucked me back in, almost instantly. I was back in love, waiting impatiently and anxiously every day to call and hear his voice. I couldn't focus on treatment. I could only focus on repairing our relationship and our love.

I swear, I must get more stupid and more gullible with age.

We agreed that I would move back in with him once I completed treatment, which would be in three months. We were going to start over.

During those three months, he swore he had changed. He promised that he had quit smoking (which I had always thought was a disgusting habit), drinking (for my sake), and doing drugs (thank God). He swore that he had been going to a therapist and to Al-Anon meetings. He swore that he was addressing his own issues as well. He promised me that he would NEVER call the police on me again, that we would talk and work anything out. He says that if we can get past this, we can get past anything, and there's nothing that could ever come between us. He told me he wanted to marry me and give me babies. He said he wanted to take care of me.

Yep … hook, line, and sinker.

Throughout my stay, we exchanged long, loving letters and cards, declaring our love for one another. He would include song lyrics from our favorite love songs, and I would just melt. He would write the most romantic things to me, and I would just fall deeper.

Yes, he's a charmer.

More like a wolf in sheep's clothing.

So on January 4, 2013, after I spent Thanksgiving, my birthday, Christmas and New Year's Eve in rehab, I was discharged.

WHOOOO HOOOO! FREE AT LAST!!

I hopped on a train and headed straight to New Haven, Connecticut, where he would be waiting for me to pick me up.

Now, Rob had advised me against moving back in with him so soon, before the PFA was lifted. But stubborn and in love, little ol' me didn't listen. After all, D had even managed to win the trust of my sister Lori, who had been my guardian angel through this entire stint in rehab. She was also convinced that he had changed, and everything was going to be fantastic. The two of them spoke on the phone every night and developed a close relationship. She was his shoulder to cry on, as well as mine.

Lori is the best. She's very wise and compassionate, but will tell you like it is and not pull and punches. She's a tough one to get by. She doesn't take any shit. She assured me that he loved me; he had changed, and badly wanted me back home with him.

I arrived at the train station after a grueling six hours on the train, to be welcomed into my love's arms, and I was home.

Finally.

CHAPTER 34
SLEEPING WITH THE ENEMY

"He was oppressed and treated harshly, yet he never said a word. He was led like a lamb to the slaughter. And as a sheep is silent before the shearers, he did not open his mouth. Unjustly condemned, he was led away."—Isaiah 53:7—8

If anyone ever tells you to take the advice of your attorney, because he is probably right, then **for God's sake, listen to them**!

January 4, I was home. Two days later, we had to attend D's grandmother's funeral. On the way home from Long Island, he pulled out a little black box.

"I had planned the perfect way to do this, but I can't wait any longer," he said. "Will you marry me?"

After a tear rolled down my cheek, I said, "Of course I will," and he placed the ring on my finger.

I'd like to say it was the most beautiful and brilliant diamond ring I had ever seen, but sadly, it wasn't. I didn't care. I loved it, because I loved him. He didn't make a lot of money, so it didn't matter to me how big or expensive it was or wasn't. It was the symbol of his unconditional love for me.

We were now engaged. Officially. It was the first time in my life someone officially proposed to me. Of course I was going to say yes. What else should I say? No? (Maybe that would have been a wiser choice).

When we got home, we made love like two people planning to spend forever with each other.

After all, that's what he would sign his letters with

Love, Forever, D——

On January 9, we went to court and the PFA was modified from Full to Limited. D stood in front of the judge and begged her to lift it completely, stating that he wanted us to go on with our lives together and our future. The judge lifted it partially, promising to remove it completely at our next scheduled court date.

We celebrated in his car after court. We were one step closer in the right direction, one step closer to being finished with all the court bullshit.

The next couple of weeks were amazing. We painted the apartment, got all new furniture, and redecorated. We tried to erase all the bad memories that occurred there by making it fresh and new. We turned it into "our home," a place where we could start fresh and new. And I **did** see the changes in him. He wasn't smoking, drinking, or using drugs. He was home on time from work every day. He blocked the bitch's number from his cell phone and blocked her from his Facebook page. He was acting more like a husband than a boyfriend. We were trying tirelessly to get pregnant.

I had no urge to drink. Not one teeny bit. None.
Until …
We were at the gym on a Wednesday night,

January 23. We were almost done with our workout, when he left my side, walked halfway across the gym floor and greeted two women with hugs, kisses, and smiles. One looked to be in her 50's and the other one was a chubby girl in her late teens.

I let him have a couple minutes of chat time, and then I walked over to be introduced. He waited. About a minute passed, as I still stood there like a dumbass with a half-assed smile on my face.

Finally, he turned and gestured toward me.

"Oh this is my girlfriend, Tammy."

He was hesitant.

What the fuck was going on? Who were these people? Why was he acting so strange around them?

They finished their little pow-wow, and hugged and kissed again, and we parted ways. When we got back to our machine, I asked who they were.

Naturally I was going to ask, right? After all, these two women were just all lovey-dovey with my fiancée for a few minutes.

He was hesitant, again.

Then with his head down and a sigh, said, "That was her mother and sister."

What the **flying mother fucking fuck**!

Are you kidding me right now? It was bad enough we saw her aunt and uncle at the gym on a nightly basis, but now he's all chummy with the whole friggin' family? Oh no, this was not happening. We left the gym immediately, with me in a fury.

The whole way home I flipped out. I went off. Could we not get this home-wrecking bitch out of our lives? Every time I turned around, there was something else to remind us of her.

I couldn't take it anymore.

We went home, and continued to argue. How could he act the way he did with them? How could he completely disrespect me in front of them? How could he not have the balls to introduce me as his fucking fiancée to them? **How could he**?

We went to bed, and Thursday I woke up just as angry. I sent him off to work and I did my best to put it out of my head. I did, for the most part, and got through my day. That evening we had an appointment at a new gym so we wouldn't bump into any more family members.

Then I got the call. He had to "Work late."

Remember what happened the last time he had to work late? **Exactly**.

So I got a case of the "fuck its" and got a little vodka.

Between last night and now this bullshit, I didn't care. I was **pissed**.

I had a couple drinks, nothing crazy, and when he came home, we got into it again. This time he backhanded me and busted my top lip open. Then he threw me down on the bed, held me down by my throat, slapped me again, ripped my clothes off and forced himself on me.

Was this rough make-up sex that he was accustomed to having? Or a sexual assault?

There is such a fine line.

When he was done, I was hurt. Battered. Bruised. Sore.

I cried myself to sleep.

I barely woke up the next day as he got ready for work. I didn't get out of bed to make his breakfast and lunch like I usually did. I lay there, sad. I slept until about noon and woke up in pain to a text from him saying, "Time to get up and start your day."

Yeah, start my day with a swollen, blackened lip and a sore neck. Wonderful.

So I did what every normal recovering alcoholic would do to relieve themselves from the pain. I drank. I self-medicated the emotional and physical pain that I was feeling.

Again, I didn't over-do it. I self-medicated, although that's never a good excuse for a relapse.

He came home from work around 6:00 p.m. He was late again, so what happened? We fought, again. This time, he tried to turn all the blame on me, saying that my drinking was the cause of our fight. But didn't he realize that it was **his** actions that caused my drinking?

I never, ever had the urge to pick up a bottle for any other reason, except when she came back into our lives, somehow, or when he got violent.

So we argued, argued and argued. We were now face to face in the kitchen when he hauled off and punched me in my left side, straight to my ribs. I dropped to the floor instantly with a pain so fierce, I couldn't breathe.

I crawled over to the couch and sat down as he got in my face.

"You're ugly," he said in a low, ugly tone, a tone dripping with sadism and hate. "I can do so much better than you."

This was coming from the man who asked me to marry him just 20 short days ago.

As I struggled to breathe and tears streamed down

my face, he walked out of the apartment. A little while later, about 30 minutes or so, my phone rang. It was my neighbor. She told me there were cops outside.

What the fuck did he do!?

Well, what he did was go straight to the police station and say that I was in the apartment and I wasn't supposed to be there, per the protective order.

Mother fucker. He did it again!

I hid in the shower, but he had given the cops a key, so they let themselves in and found me.

Arrest number six.

I was in the apartment and wasn't supposed to be there? This came from the man who begged me to come back home and to forgive him. This from the man who rented a moving truck and drove to New Jersey to my mother's house to move all my things back to Connecticut. This from the man who put a ring on my finger and asked me to be his wife. This from the man who was trying his damnedest, six times a day, to start a family with me. This from the man who agreed that if we ever had a fight, we'd cool off separately and never involve the law again.

This from the man whom I gave my total and complete trust to **again** when all signs told me I shouldn't.

You know how that old saying goes: Fool me once, shame on you. Fool me twice, shame on me.

Another three nights in a holding cell, $100,000 cash bond, and two broken ribs later, I was carted off to prison. Again.

But not before I got X-rays to prove my injuries and gave a written statement of his abuse.

Oh, by the way, did I mention that this all

257

happened on January 25? Our eight-month anniversary? Oh yeah. Happy anniversary to me.

So here I sit, Inmate #393257 of the Connecticut State Penal System.

SHATTERED.

CHAPTER 35
SO MUCH FOR MY HAPPY ENDING

So much for my happy ending. Six little words couldn't be truer right now.

You know the expression "Be careful what you wish for?" Take heed in that, as I should have just eight short months earlier.

I was wishing for the fairy tale, the happy ending, my Knight in Shining Armor. I wanted a husband, a family, a cute little house with a white picket fence and two dogs.

Boy, did I choose the wrong guy for that, right?

I didn't see it before, though. When I met him, I was blinded by an undying love. Or was it just lust and really good sex? At first I thought it was love, but now that fine line between love and lust was beginning to blur.

If it was just lust, no wonder it went so far south that Satan had to designate a catcher. Lust **is** one of the seven deadly sins, after all. I must have taken one too many bites from the forbidden fruit for my own good.

As I sat there in jail writing the previous chapters, I began to realize that there was never any stability to our relationship. My trust was blown out of the water by his cheating and it never came back (although I tried so hard to forgive and trust again). I overlooked so many of his faults because I was so desperate to be **"in love."** I had such a need to be loved by someone and live a "normal life" of marriage, babies, etc., that I jumped at the first thing that presented itself to me.

Throughout the month of January, leading up to this last arrest, I did notice some things that were quite alarming.

When I would talk about stepping away from the business completely to focus on going back to school, he would get really upset.

When I said I would take some bookings for autograph signings but not to manage him on shows, he got highly offended.

When I said we would not be attending the Hall of Fame or WrestleMania that spring, he was pissed off because he wanted the backstage access I could give him and his friends.

When I made $3,000 cash fast to clear up his overdue and past due rent and bills, he loved me more.

I learned, through a nightly ritual of sharing things about each other, that he was more promiscuous than I had ever imagined or feared; or even wanted to hear about. I can't even bring myself to share the details with you!

I learned that he really had no intention of remaining smoke, alcohol, and drug-free for the sake of our relationship.

I learned that he was completely content with living off his soon-to-be wife since he had zero ambition to better himself or support himself on his own. I learned that he was telling promoters that I would only work for them, if he got booked on the show as well.

When I would slack in writing this book, he got furious that the "big payday" would be delayed even further, as he was counting on the profit from this book to pay for our wedding.

When I sit back and take this all in, I say to myself, **"What were you thinking, you crazy bitch?!**

Honestly, I **do** think that, even out loud sometimes!

The forbidden fruit. Yep. It got a hold of me good.

Was this God's way of teaching me something? Was it His way of teaching me about lust and greed?

They say that everything happens for a reason, but I'm STILL trying to figure out what **this** reason is.

Is it that God knew D wasn't the right one for me? Is it so I stop drinking once and for all? Is it a combination of all of it?

I don't know. I just don't know.

I'd like to now share a bit of the daily journal I kept while in jail at this time.

FRIDAY, FEBRUARY 15, 2013, APPROX. 3:00 P.M.

I'm still waiting for my lawyer, Rob, to show up to visit. He said he was coming last night, but I'm still waiting … waiting.

7:00 P.M.

Oh well, Rob's a no-show. Something must have come up. He has become a good friend and confidante; he wouldn't just blow me off.

WEDNESDAY, MARCH 13, 2013, 6:00 P.M.

Well, I went to court yesterday. Nothing eventful, but I presented my new lawyer to the court. Rob was forced out of the case by the prosecution, so he found me someone to take over. I hope he's decent! All that's left in the case is the pre-sentence investigation and my sentencing.

I want to be sentenced already to get it over with, but I'm also terrified to get sentenced. I almost feel better NOT knowing my fate. Not knowing how long I have to be here in jail. I have six weeks of lock-up already under my belt, so that will count towards whatever I get sentenced to.

Because this charge is a five-year felony, I am realistically looking at a possible three to five years in jail.

I'm also stressed out because D will not return calls to my mother and sister about them moving my things out of the apartment.

I already have enough to worry about, and now I have that on my mind!

Everything I own is there with him. I'm nervous about losing everything. After screwing up the last year of my life, he better do the right thing by me and get my stuff to my mother's house.

THURSDAY, MARCH 14, 2013, 8:00 P.M.

This jail thing is getting monotonous. I tried calling Rob to tell him the book is just about finished, but he's not picking up the phone … grrr.

The food here is terrible, so you have to figure out meals to make with your commissary food and using the hot water pot as an oven. Tonight was chicken parm and pepperoni wraps—not too shabby for what I have to work with. You kind of turn into a modern day MacGyver in jail. You can make anything out of nothing.

It kind of feels like you are in a college dorm the way rooms are set up. For the most part everyone gets along. The part that really sucks is having to poop right in front of your Bunkie (roommate). No privacy at all!

I was in a group tonight, and the topic was "love." I'm the type of person that loves being in love, loves being loved, and loves to love someone. But after this last disaster at an attempt of being in love, I wonder if it's all worth the hassle.

If being in love brings you heartache, headaches, and in my case, jail, is it really all worth it?

I don't know anymore.

I think I might just stay single for a while.

SATURDAY, MARCH 16, 2013, 1:24 P.M.

I was just taking a nap, when the corrections officer buzzed my room and told me I had a job here at the prison. The job is in the kitchen, not sure doing what yet, but I know I'll be making a whopping 75 cents per day! Whooo! I'm gonna be rich!

Kitchen workers get 75 cents a day, laundry workers get $1.20, and seamstresses make 35 cents an hour.

Yes, it's a sweatshop.

Oh, did I forget to mention I have to wake up at 3:30 a.m.?

Yep. A sweatshop.

Rob should be coming to visit tomorrow. I have

to give him the last two notebooks I wrote of this book so he can type them up for publishing. There are 460 pages so far to type up, so he definitely has some work cut out for him.

I spoke to my mom last night. She's sending a moving company up to D's apartment on Saturday, the 23rd, to get all of my things. It's about time. He's been holding it all hostage for seven weeks now. He wasn't returning anyone's phone calls at all. He continues to prove to be a scumbag.

All I know is it all better be there, not broken, either. If it is, I'll sue his ass in court ... not that he has any money to sue for.

As soon as all my things are at my mom's, I can finally wash my hands of him completely. It's about time. None of us will ever have to speak to him again. And mark my words—if he ever shows up at a wrestling event I'm working, I'll have his ass tossed out fast!

SUNDAY, MARCH 17TH, 2013, 6:30 P.M.

Well, today was my first day of work in the kitchen. I prepared trays for breakfast, then washed pans all day. It was the hardest $ .75 I've ever made. If jail is supposed to humble you, it's doing its job.

SATURDAY, MARCH 23, 2013, 6:00 P.M.

Well, we were bored today, so my Bunkie Sherri wanted to do something crazy, so we shaved half of her head! HA!

TUESDAY, MARCH 26, 2013, 11:30 A.M.

Well it's been an eventful couple of days.

On Sunday, I got fired from my kitchen job. Yep, I lasted one whole week! They caught me taking cake out of the kitchen, which is a big no-no. I was bringing it back to make a birthday cake for a girl on my tier. So I got caught and fired. Oh well.

I don't think I'll miss the hard labor for that whopping 75 cents a day.

This morning I had a visit from probation. I had to tell her the whole story from start to finish about everything that has happened for the pre-sentence investigation. Basically she said she doesn't think I need jail time, and she is going to recommend just probation.

Yay!! Things are finally starting to turn around.

I have court next Tuesday, the 2nd, but it will just be continued. She said my sentencing will be in May, so I'll be here another month. C'est la vie.

I'm also a bit agitated that I haven't been able to call Rob in over a week. Something screwy is going on with the phones, and I can't get through to him ... grr.

WEDNESDAY, MARCH 27, 2013

Ahhh! Jail **can** get worse!!

I had to go in front of the disciplinary review board because I stole the cake from the kitchen. My punishment is Loss of Commissary for 30 days.

Thirty days?

That means no candy, no cookies, no brownies, no oatmeal cream pies, and no chips—nothing from commissary. How will I survive?

I don't know, I guess it's a blessing. I wanted to drop a few pounds before I leave here anyway.

I told my sister I had the meeting with the

probation officer and that I'll probably get out in four or five weeks. Now it's time to plan my next step. I think I'll go to her house in Pennsylvania for a couple weeks and then move out to New Mexico with my brother.

He has a big, beautiful home with a two-bedroom apartment above his garage. I'll go out there for about a year, get a job, and be normal for a change.

After that, when this book comes out, I think I'll retire to San Diego, buy a nice condo on the beach and open a breakfast and lunch café.

Sounds like heaven.

CHAPTER 36
THE BIG 'C'

Today has not been a good day.

I got some really bad news this morning, and I'm pretty upset about it.

When I first got to prison, I had a gynecological exam and a Pap smear done, since I was almost due for my annual exam anyway. The Pap smear came back positive for abnormal cells—namely HPV.

The Human Papillomavirus is a sexually transmitted disease carried and transmitted by men, but it afflicts women. There are no symptoms, but when left untreated, the abnormal HPV cells can turn into cervical cancer cells.

After I tested positive for HPV, I had a biopsy done, something called a colposcopy, to further investigate how far advanced these abnormal cells were.

There are three different strains of HPV: one that clears up on its own, a second that causes genital warts and a third that can progress to pre-cancerous cells. The pre-cancerous cells, if caught early enough, can be frozen and scraped off of the cervix, but if left untreated will eventually progress into cancer cells.

Well, this morning, my colposcopy results came back positive for Cervical Squamous Cell Carcinoma.

In layman's terms, I have cervical cancer.

Yep, at 40 years old, I have cancer.

I cried like a baby when I first found out, but now I'm just in shock and disbelief.

How did I get cancer?

Well, like I said, you get it from sexual contact with a man. My last Pap smear was one year ago, and it was negative for any abnormal cells.

Since then, I have only had one sexual partner, so you can do the math.

Fortunately, cervical cancer is treatable, but invasive and severe.

I will be going to the University of Connecticut Medical Center to have surgery, a cone biopsy. They will be putting me under general anesthetic, and cutting a cone shaped chunk out of my cervix. Hopefully they get all the cancer cells out that way.

If they don't get all the cells out—if the cells extend up into the uterus or if the cancer is too progressed—I will need a hysterectomy.

Also, the cone biopsy is a very bloody procedure they say, so if I bleed too much or if the bleeding doesn't stop, they'll have to do a hysterectomy right then and there, without me even knowing.

I never wanted to have a child until this past year, and now, after the cone biopsy, there will be only a one percent chance that I can ever get pregnant.

And if they do a hysterectomy, well then, I'll never have a child of my own.

So, needless to say, I'm pretty fucking upset. This is a life-changing event for me, no matter what.

I hope the treatment is the lesser of the two, and that it will be all I need, but I'm scared shitless. I asked the doctor what would happen if I decided not to get it treated. "You'll endure a very slow, very painful death," she said.

She said the pain from cervical cancer death is right up there with pancreatic cancer. It will kill you, and it will hurt tremendously.

When will this madness end? Will I ever just be able to live a normal and happy life?

What the hell have I done to deserve all this strife and heartache?

I have been a good and generous person all my life. I've donated thousands of dollars to animal rescue groups. I've been polite and kind to everyone who crosses my path. I've always taken care of others needs before my own.

And I get cursed with Cancer.

Me. Cancer.

Let this be a lesson to myself and all of you women reading this: **always** use a condom. No matter what, or who. It will save your cervix, and your life.

WEDNESDAY, APRIL 3, 2013, 10:30 A.M.

Court was yesterday. I met my new lawyer, Rose. Real nice lady.

She met with the prosecutor. He's pushing for three years! Is he insane?

Then Rose met with the judge. The judge was sympathetic towards me, thank God, and Rose said she is "on my side."

Whew!

I'm still hoping and praying that I only get

probation, but there's still that one percent chance I may have to sit here in jail a little longer.

MONDAY, APRIL 8, 2013, 4 P.M.

I've been thinking about D a lot today. Probably because we were supposed to attend a wedding next weekend and WrestleMania was this past weekend.

I wonder who he will be taking to the wedding? Not that I'm jealous in any way, I just wonder.

I wonder what it would be like to go with him?

Then I can't stop thinking three things:

1) He's a liar.
2) He's a cheater
3) He's a broke-ass loser

OK. I'm over it.

FRIDAY, APRIL 12, 8:00 P.M.

Just got back from the hospital and my first real appointment about my cancer. It finally hit home when they wheeled me into the Cancer Unit at UCONN. The cancer unit! Oh my God. I never thought I'd ever be a patient there. It really is a scary thing, you know? Ok, maybe you don't know.

In my appointment with my amazing doctor, we discussed my options. Basically, the cone biopsy isn't the best way to go. Too many risks and complications can arise. She wants to do the hysterectomy the first time in.

Oh God, a hysterectomy. She said it's the best way to make sure all the cancer is out of me, and if we get it all now, I shouldn't need any radiation or chemotherapy.

I can't believe this. Any hope I ever had of having a family is slowly slipping through my fingertips. I'm even more in shock now than ever.

After my appointment, I went back into the waiting room and realized I have my period right now. This is going to be the last period I'm **ever** going to have. Then I looked up at the TV and an actor was on Ellen DeGeneres talking about his new baby girl … named Olivia. Well, wasn't that just a shot through the heart, because that's what I always wanted to name my daughter, if I ever had one.

Man, all these thoughts and feelings running through me are out of control. I haven't really been that distraught over the surgery until now. It's really starting to hit home. Hard.

MONDAY, APRIL 29, 2013, 7:00 P.M.

I just came back from the hospital. They did all my pre-surgery stuff—physical, EKG, blood work. All my blood work was perfect! I'm in complete perfect health! My liver enzymes couldn't be better; my white and red cell counts are right on target. I'm as healthy as a horse internally. So how the hell did I develop cancer?

Some things are just out of your control. It doesn't matter how healthy you eat or how much you exercise. Medical problems can hit anyone at any time. Cancer knows no boundaries.

FAST FORWARD TO DECEMBER 2015………..

I finally sat back down to write, because May through December of this year has been a crazy roller coaster. My hysterectomy is complete... after two surgeries. Yes, two! A DaVinci Robot did my first surgery and, wouldn't you know it… **It screwed up**! I had **cervical cancer**, and the robot and doctor left part of my cervix in! During this time, I was released from prison after the judge dropped the charges against me, and I went to a new oncologist. He performed a second surgery, removing the remainder of my cervix, an inch of my vagina, 26 pelvic lymph nodes, and all the ligaments that used to hold my uterus to my pelvic bones.

I am home, recovering from this second, and much more painful, surgery and I still can't believe this has all happened to me in the course of one year.

At least the worst is over…It's over.

My tissues came back from Pathology, and I am officially cancer-free. I don't need any radiation or chemotherapy, which the doctors had originally assumed that I would need. I'm out of the water…At least for now. And I thank God every day for that.

CHAPTER 37
A NEW LEASE ON LIFE

It is 2015. My cancer is gone. Prison is behind me. What now? What have I done since 2013?

Well, being off the 'wrestling' scene through the duration of my cancer and surgeries did set me back a bit. I was living with my sister through recovery, not working, and depleting what savings I had throughout the year. I started taking phone calls from fans through a service called "Verified Calls" during my recovery, as a way to have some income while I was pretty much house-bound. Fans would purchase a block of time to talk to me on the phone, and at the end of the month, I would get a check from the company. This was doing well for a while, although I was taking in well under $1,000 per month, but at least it was giving me a little spending money so I wouldn't have to rely solely on my sister.

One night, I had a brainstorm. If people were paying their hard-earned money to talk to me on the phone, what would they pay to talk to me **and** see me???

So I got the idea to start Skype video chats. I set up my Skype account, and advertised on social media that I was taking video calls... Strictly question and answer sessions. It started as X amount of dollars for X amount of minutes, and wasn't a lot… At first.

I was getting Q&A calls for about six months, completely innocent chats. Until one night, when out of nowhere, a male fan decided to whip it out. Yes, he took his male reproductive organ out of his pants. "OMG,!!" I thought, "What in the world is going on??"

Yep. He pretty much just wanted to look at me and masturbate. **Right there on camera!** He just whipped it out and started whacking off… "OMG." I couldn't believe what I was seeing.

Then a light bulb lit up over my shocked and confused little head…

If these guys want to look at me and relieve themselves, I can wear a little less and charge a little more. Hell, I can wear **a lot** less and charge **a lot** more!!!

So what began as a simple, fully-clothed, Q&A session with a fan, turned into an all-out sexual, skin revealing, wank-fest for a lot more money… Ha-ha, some guys will do anything!

I do joke about it, but honestly, I appreciate every single one of my customers. I see nothing wrong with what I, or they, do I've always been a very sexual person, a bit of an exhibitionist and voyeur, and this was just another way for me to explore my sexuality. After two and a half years of Skyping and building up my business, it has become as large as it is today, and I have about 50 returning customers from all over the world: the US, Canada, England, Ireland, Scotland, Germany, Portugal, India, Japan, Australia, and even Iraq. I won't discuss how much money I take in by Skyping, but I will say that I make more than double weekly what the WWE used to pay me to be out on the road full time. **Plus**, I had road expenses then! Now, I work out of my home... My bedroom is my office and my bed is my desk. What could be better! I am my own boss, make my own hours, enjoy what I do, and have the best and easiest job in the world! What could possibly top this!?

Well, there is **one** thing that could top it... And many would say it's the natural progression of the business... Namely entertainment with a sexual overtone...

In December 2014, I received a series of emails from a specific company wanting to do business with me. I simply chalked it up to a fan messing around with me through emails, so I ignored them. But after about eight unanswered emails, I decided to investigate further.

These emails were from a woman named Jackie from Vivid Entertainment. Yes, Vivid. The porn company. No, wait, excuse me, the **!!biggest porn company in the world!** These emails repeatedly stated that Vivid was interested in doing a movie with me.

Yeah, Okay. A movie. Vivid Video wants me to do a movie. Whatever. I mean, I even turned down *Playboy* in 1996. There is no way I can film a porno, even if these were legitimate emails.

So one day, I humored them and wrote them back. The reply I received was, "Yes, this is Vivid Video and we would like to feature you in a celebrity sex tape."

What? Wait...**What!!!!?**

Oh my God. Is this a joke? Me? In a celebrity sex tape?

My first thought was "no." "Hell no!" There was no way I could do this. For a few reasons;

1) I had never had sex in front of anyone before... Ever.

275

2) I had never allowed anyone to film me having sex, for obvious reasons. As soon as I would have dumped the guy, the tape would surely be released all over the Internet.

For about three weeks I was going back and forth... thinking, "Yeah, maybe I could do this," and "No, there's no Goddamn way..."

Finally, I got on the phone with the big boss man, Steven Hirsch himself, the owner of Vivid Entertainment. He explained to me how they would film it, how it would be marketed, and that I could choose with whom I wanted to film.

After all of these conversations with Steven, I was still on the fence about it, definitely leaning towards the "no" side of the fence. Then during one phone call, Steven said, "Well, let me send you a sample contract. Read it and see what we have to offer you, then get back to me."

They forwarded me the contract. I was nervous just to open the email and read it!!

But I did. I read it. Then I read it again.

My next thought and question was, 'Okay, where do I sign?"

This contract, and the offer that Vivid made me, was unbelievable. Almost too good to be true. Was this really happening to me? For me? Was I getting the chance of a lifetime, after 25 years of hard work and busting my ass in the wrestling business? After 25 years of ups and downs, making money and losing it, being wealthy and being broke, was I finally getting the chance to turn my financial well being around and live a secure and prosperous life?

Once again, I'm not going into numbers here...

But with the offer they made me, and the right investments, I can **totally** set myself up to be comfortable... And enjoy life for a change.

So I signed the contract. I was now officially under a legally binding contract to make celebrity porn for Vivid Entertainment. Oh my God.... Shit was about to change!!

Long story short, and I won't go into all the gory details, but I filmed the movie. My two co-stars were professionals, Derrick Pierce and Will Powers. And let me tell you. I give these guys, and all performers and crew in the adult film business, all the credit in the world. This shit's not easy!! It took 13 hours to get 120 minutes of usable footage on film!! Thirteen hours!! It was the longest day of my life! And if you think I had it rough, getting banged for 13 hours, just imagine the guys!! I filmed six hours with each one, and I have to hand it to them... they each kept it up for SIX **straight hours**! God only knows how... Well, God and the companies that make Cialis and Viagra, I assume... Ha!

And the craziest part of working with all of these new people... I found that the actors and office personnel and crewmembers are some of the most professional and kind people I've ever worked with! The porn industry has this stigma that they are a seedy, shady business... And granted, maybe many of them are. But Vivid Entertainment blew me away with their professionalism and courtesy. They put the WWE and wrestling business to shame when it comes to how they treat their performers. There really is no comparison. Totally blew me away.

So, it's in the books. It's official. Sunny made a porno. The Original Diva of the WWE and WWE Hall of Famer has made an adult film. "OH MY GOD." I have officially done the craziest thing I could possibly ever do.

Craziest, and most brilliant.

So now, the wait has begun for the release of the film…the long, much-anticipated wait. Cover art work done…Check. Trailer done… Check. PR statements done… Check.

What's next for Tam? Well, the movie will come out in a few short weeks from now, and I have plans to start up a new Skype website, managing various male and female models underneath me. I have big ideas; I just need to work hard to bring them all to fruition.

Of course I expect all the negative criticism in the world from media, fans, friends and family everywhere. I know it's coming. It's expected. It's welcomed. I have never shied away from the press and media, and I'm not about to start. After almost 26 years in the entertainment business, I have traded in my skin for a coating of Kevlar… **Nothing** can penetrate this outer shell and get to me. Through all my struggles and strife in life, I have managed to keep my head above water, and when all else fails, I resort back to what always works for me…. Being true to myself and working hard to be the best person I can be. I know that with my determination and perseverance, I will always survive. Survival of the fittest. That's how I live my life. And always will.

So how and why did this all happen to me? Only God knows why… But I'll never stop trying to figure it all out.

EPILOGUE

Six years.

That is how long it took for me to write this book.

I had the idea six years ago, but didn't know the message I wanted to convey until I ended up in prison.

Everything I've gone through has made me appreciate life so much more—my successful career, my battle with alcoholism, my "glorious" stint in jail and my bout with cancer.

What I wanted to express to everyone is that I am human. I am just like every one of you. I'm not any more special than the person next to me just because I have been famous.

Everyone makes mistakes. Nobody is perfect. But when you've been blessed with success and good things all your life, and then you do one thing wrong, it is viewed as an earth-shattering tragedy—a fall from grace.

I have been abused, ridiculed, harassed, imprisoned and blasted in the media for making the same mistakes that everyone in this world makes.

Nobody's perfect.

My hope is that you, in reading this book, can find solace and peace within yourselves, as I have done. Writing this book has allowed me to analyze my life, and has given me a great sense of closure. Sometimes a little closure is what is needed in your life to feel fulfilled.

Through yoga, meditation and religion, I have found peace within myself and finally, at 43 years old, I am comfortable in my own skin.

I know now that there is no challenge too great for me to conquer, no mountain too high.

Struggling is a part of life. How you handle it is what makes the difference.

My stint in jail taught me a lot. It is absolutely mind-blowing how many good women are in prison for multi-year sentences because of a man. My second roommate Sherri, for example, is serving a 25-year sentence for first degree murder. The thing is, **she** didn't kill anyone. Her boyfriend did, and because he scared the bejesus out of her, she got the same charge because she didn't give him up to the police.

It's sad.

Too many women in prison are victims. They are victims of abuse, rape and manipulation, and they are suffering consequences that they shouldn't have to. experiencing.

What the world needs are more activists to get the justice system to see its faults and to not punish innocent women for the crimes their men commit. These women are terrified to stand up for themselves and threatened by their men if they do.

If anything, these women need to be placed into programs to build their self-esteem and self-worth. They need help to build their inner strength to deal with the obstacles they face in their lives.

I know this … I **am** one of those women.

What the world has in store for me from this point forward is yet to be seen. I'm sure it **all** won't be a walk through the tulips or a bed of roses, but I can only hope for the best. That's all I can do.

As long as I remain determined and persevere, nothing can stop me. My faith and passion will steer me in the right directions, and with a little help from my Kevlar skin, I'm shooting for the stars….

And besides, we've all known since 1996, that 'what Sunny wants, Sunny gets!!'

About the Author

The legendary Sunny is known as "the original **WWE Diva"** and she is one of the most popular female wrestling personalities of all time. Her achievements include being a two time **Slammy Award Winner,** a member of the **WWE Hall of Fame** and **New England Pro Wrestling Hall of Fame** and **a Pro Wrestling Illustrated Manager of the Year. Other Riverdale Avenue Books You Might Like**

Acknowledgments

This book would not be possible without the help, support and encouragement of the following people:

All the wonderful men and women I met, learned from and befriended in my two decades in wrestling;

My wonderful family who have stood by me through thick and thin;

The incredible team at Vivid Entertainment, especially Jackie, Marci and Steven;

My first editor, Dan Murphy, who really believed in this book, and my team of editors at Riverdale Avenue Books.

Other Books From Riverdale Avenue Books

Unphiltered: Life On and Off the Rock'n'Roll Tour Bus
By Phil Varone

The Making of Going for the Gold
By Taylor Lianne Chandler and Lissa Trevor

Lindsay Lohan: Fully Loaded, From Disney to Disaster
By Marc Shapiro

Flashes: Adventures in Dating Through Menopause
By Michelle Churchill

Confessions of a Librarian – A Memoir of Loves
By Barbara Foster